# ANTHOLOGY

*— for —*

## MUSIC IN THE EIGHTEENTH CENTURY

**Western Music in Context: A Norton History**

Walter Frisch  SERIES EDITOR

*Music in the Medieval West,* by Margot Fassler

*Music in the Renaissance,* by Richard Freedman

*Music in the Baroque,* by Wendy Heller

*Music in the Eighteenth Century,* by John Rice

*Music in the Nineteenth Century,* by Walter Frisch

*Music in the Twentieth and Twenty-First Centuries,* by Joseph Auner

# ANTHOLOGY

*— for —*

## MUSIC IN THE EIGHTEENTH CENTURY

John Rice

W. W. NORTON AND COMPANY

NEW YORK · LONDON

W. W. Norton & Company has been independent since its founding in 1923, when William Warder Norton and Mary D. Herter Norton first published lectures delivered at the People's Institute, the adult education division of New York City's Cooper Union. The firm soon expanded its program beyond the Institute, publishing books by celebrated academics from America and abroad. By midcentury, the two major pillars of Norton's publishing program—trade books and college texts—were firmly established. In the 1950s, the Norton family transferred control of the company to its employees, and today—with a staff of four hundred and a comparable number of trade, college, and professional titles published each year—W. W. Norton & Company stands as the largest and oldest publishing house owned wholly by its employees.

Editor: Maribeth Payne
Associate Editor: Justin Hoffman
Assistant Editor: Ariella Foss
Developmental Editor: Harry Haskell
Manuscript Editor: JoAnn Simony
Project Editor: Jack Borrebach
Electronic Media Editor: Steve Hoge
Marketing Manager, Music: Amy Parkin
Production Manager: Ashley Horna
Photo Editor: Stephanie Romeo
Permissions Manager: Megan Jackson
Text Design: Jillian Burr
Composition: CM Preparé
Manufacturing: Quad/Graphics-Fairfield, PA

W. W. Norton & Company, Inc., 500 Fifth Avenue, New York, NY 10110-0017
wwnorton.com
W. W. Norton & Company, Ltd., Castle House, 75/76 Wells Street, London W1T3QT

1 2 3 4 5 6 7 8 9 0

1. 4
2. 3
3. 1
4. 2
5. 6
~~6. 4~~ 6:9
7. 5
8. 9
9 - 7
~~10. 10~~

(30-49)

listen in chronological order.

(Areas)

1760)
(1750-1770

(1760-1790)

# CONTENTS

# PREFACE

This anthology accompanies *Music in the Eighteenth Century*, part of the series Western Music in Context: A Norton History. The anthology includes scores and analytical commentary for a broad range of compositions, from music that composers under the spell of the new galant style wrote in Italy during the late 1720s and 1730s to music that Haydn and Beethoven wrote in Vienna in the first decade of the nineteenth century. Selections appear in the order in which they are discussed in *Music in the Eighteenth Century* (which is often, but not always, chronological).

In choosing music for the anthology I have tried to strike a reasonable balance between instrumental and vocal and have aimed for a wide variety of genres, both sacred and secular. The anthology includes numbers from both comic and serious operas and movements from concertos, symphonies, keyboard sonatas, and string quartets. One of my goals in choosing instrumental movements has been to exemplify as many different forms as possible. Readers will find examples of parallel and rounded binary form, sonata form, theme and variations, and rondo.

In order to maximize the amount of music in this anthology, I have presented vocal works (and one concerto movement) with the accompaniment reduced to two staves. Some of these items are normal piano-vocal scores, with the orchestral accompaniment arranged as an idiomatic piano part. In others, my main goal has been to preserve—as much as possible on two staves—the orchestra's figuration and part-writing, even where this resulted in occasional passages that are not playable on the piano.

Each selection in the anthology is followed by analytic commentary and—in the case of vocal music—the text in the original language and in translation. I do not intend the commentary to be exhaustive or definitive, but to encourage readers to explore the music in depth.

In order to clarify the music's formal structure, I have illustrated the commentary with many diagrams, most of which contain the words "First Part" and "Second Part." With these I refer to the two basic parts of binary form, to which eighteenth-century musicians often referred (using Italian) as the *prima parte* and the *seconda parte*, or (to use the terminology of Heinrich Christoph Koch) the first section and the second section. By employing "First Part" and "Second Part" as formal categories throughout this anthology, I hope to emphasize the extent to which eighteenth-century composers, whether they were writing sacred music, opera, or instrumental music, depended on binary form in all its wonderful variety and potential for elaboration.

A wide range of recording options gives students and instructors flexibility in listening to anthology selections. StudySpace, Norton's online resource for students, provides links to stream most anthology selections from the Naxos Music Library (accessible via an institutional or individual subscription), as well as links to purchase and download recordings from iTunes and Amazon. The Norton Opera Sampler offers streaming Metropolitan Opera video of many opera excerpts included here.

I would like to take this opportunity to thank some of those who made this anthology possible. Allan Badley allowed me to include keyboard-vocal scores of excerpts of his editions of music by Vanhal and the Chevalier de St. Georges. Craig H. Russell gave me a copy of his edition of Jerusalem's *Matins for the Virgin of Guadalupe* and permitted me to republish an excerpt here. Bruce Alan Brown shared with me his photographs of a manuscript keyboard-vocal score of Gluck's song *Je n'amais pas tabac beaucoup*, which served as the basis of the score in the anthology. Monica S. Fazckas (University of Western Ontario) sent me a copy of part of her library's manuscript score of Traetta's *Antigona*, on which the score of Traetta's chorus *Piangi, o Tebe* is based.

# ANTHOLOGY

*— for —*

## MUSIC IN THE EIGHTEENTH CENTURY

# GIOVANNI BATTISTA PERGOLESI (1710–1736)

## Stabat Mater: Stabat mater dolorosa
### 1736

Edited by John A. Rice. Principal source: Naples, Conservatario San Pietro a Majella, Cantate 381.

| Stabat mater dolorosa | *The mournful mother stood* |
|---|---|
| Juxta crucem lacrimosa | *weeping next to the cross* |
| Dum pendebat filius. | *from which her son was hanging.* |

The medieval sequence Stabat Mater is a poetic meditation on the sorrow of Mary, the mother of Christ, at her son's crucifixion and death. Many composers set the words to music, but no setting was as famous in the eighteenth century, and as frequently performed, as the one made in 1736 by the young Giovanni Battista Pergolesi shortly before his death. His *Stabat Mater* consists of a series of duets and arias for soprano and alto, accompanied by strings. He probably intended both solo parts for castrated singers known as *musici* (or less politely as *castrati*), who dominated the performance of sacred music in Italy. (Today these solos—like the arias by Johann Adolf Hasse and Christoph Gluck to be considered later in this anthology—are sung by women or male countertenors.)

The opening movement is a duet in parallel binary form, in which orchestral passages known as ritornellos (literally, "little things that return") serve to frame the solo passages and articulate the form. After the first ritornello (or orchestral introduction) in the tonic, F minor, the first part modulates to C minor. (Pergolesi could have modulated to the relative major, Ab, but he preferred the dominant minor here in order to maintain a darker emotional color.) The second part, a setting of the same text, modulates from C minor back to F minor while presenting much of the same melodic material as the first part.

| FORM | | | First Part | | Second Part | |
|---|---|---|---|---|---|---|
| | | Rit. 1 | **A** | Rit. 2 | **A'** | Rit. 3 |
| KEY (i = F MINOR) | | i | i–v | v | v–i | i |
| TEXT (LINES) | | | 1–3 | | 1–3 | |
| MEASURES | | 1–11 | 12–26 | 27–28 | 28–45 | 46–47 |

Eighteenth-century composers, even masters of the galant style such as Pergolesi, often had recourse to the learned style when writing church music. Counterpoint had associations with antiquity, which made it appropriate for bringing to musical life Christianity's ancient rituals and eternal truths, whether those truths were Protestant or Catholic. Within the duet's binary framework, Pergolesi synthesized the learned and galant. He began both parts of the binary structure with a texture resembling that of a trio sonata (a genre cultivated primarily by composers born in the seventeenth century): two treble parts in counterpoint above a walking bass. (For an eighteenth-century example, see Domenico Gallo's Trio Sonata No. 1 in G Major, Anthology 7). The ascending chain of suspensions unfolds as a canon, with the soprano imitating the alto one step higher. But polyphony soon yields to the homophonic textures of the galant style. The orchestral cadences at the end of each part (ritornellos 2 and 3) use a bass line, on the scale degrees $\hat{3}$–$\hat{4}$–$\hat{5}$–$\hat{6}$, $\hat{3}$–$\hat{4}$–$\hat{5}$–$\hat{1}$, of which galant composers were especially fond. (Lodovico Giustini used this bass pattern in exactly the same formal context and for the same purpose: to emphasize closure at the end of both parts of a binary-form movement; see Anthology 4, mm. 25–28 and 60–63). Another typically galant element is the descending sequence in mm. 18–21, in which a passage in the minor mode (here B♭ minor) is followed by the same music a whole step lower and in the major mode (A♭ major). Eighteenth-century composers loved this particular two-step sequence, which the theorist Joseph Riepel called a "Fonte" (Italian for "spring" or "fountain").

The minor mode, a prevailing low dynamic level with occasional loud eruptions, and dissonance generated by the suspensions in the violins and vocal parts work together to convey Mary's inconsolable grief. Like many great composers of vocal music, Pergolesi knew when to take liberties with his text. At measures 41–42, he focused the listener's attention on Mary's feelings by isolating the adjectives "dolorosa" (mournful) and "lacrimosa" (weeping), and having the singers repeat them to a phrase that spans an expressive diminished seventh. With good reason did Jean-Jacques Rousseau, in his *Dictionnaire de musique* (Dictionary of Music) of 1768, call this duet "the most perfect and most touching to come from the pen of any musician."

# La serva padrona: A Serpina penserete

## 1733

Edited by John A. Rice. Principal source: Naples, Conservatario S. Pietro a Majella, Rari 7.6.13.

A Serpina penserete
 Qualche volta e qualche dì
 E direte "Ah! poverina,
 Cara un tempo ella mi fu."
 (Ei mi par che già pian piano
 S'incomincia a intenerir.)

*You will think of Serpina*
*some time, some day,*
*and you will say: "Poor lass!*
*She was once dear to me."*
*(I think he's gradually*
*beginning to soften.)*

| S'io poi fui impertinente, | *And if I was impertinent,* |
|---|---|
| Mi perdoni: malamente | *forgive me: I behaved* |
| Mi guidai, lo vedo sì. | *badly, I see it now.* |
| (Ei mi stringe per la mano, | *(He's pressing my hand:* |
| Meglio il fatto non può gir.) | *things could not be going better.)* |

In 1733 the 23-year-old Giovanni Battista Pergolesi wrote the opera seria *Il prigionier superbo* (The Proud Prisoner) for performance at the Teatro San Bartolomeo, the royal theater of Naples, in celebration of the birthday of the Habsburg empress Elizabeth Christina. (Naples at this time was under the rule of the Austrian Habsburgs.) Pergolesi also wrote an intermezzo: a miniature comic opera in two parts, to be performed during the intermissions between the three acts of *Il prigionier superbo*. With this intermezzo, *La serva padrona* (The Servant Turned Mistress), he and his librettist, Gennaro Antonio Federico, created a little masterpiece of musical comedy.

*La serva padrona* has only two singing characters, and a third character who communicates with gestures only. Serpina is a clever, pretty servant girl who hopes to charm her employer Uberto, a rich but foolish old man, into marrying her. In her aria *A Serpina penserete* (You will think of Serpina), she tells Uberto that he will be sorry when she is gone. The aria constitutes a little drama in which Serpina manipulates Uberto's feelings by expressing three different emotional states: her own feigned sadness and contrition, Uberto's future feelings as he mourns her absence, and her real feelings of sly delight, which she reveals to the audience in asides. Pergolesi ingeniously used a da capo structure as the vehicle for Serpina's display.

**Large-scale form**

| FORM | A | B | A |
|---|---|---|---|
| KEY (I = B♭) | I | iii | I |
| TEXT (LINES) | 1–6 | 7–11 | 1–6 |
| MEASURES | 1–60 | 60–77 | 1–60 |

The text is in the customary two stanzas, with the first stanza serving as the text of the **A** section and the second stanza the text of the **B** section. The **A** section, like that of Johann Adolf Hasse's *Per questo dolce amplesso* (Anthology 3), is in parallel binary form, with the first part moving from tonic B♭ to dominant F and the second part from the dominant back to the tonic. But in a striking departure from convention, Pergolesi divided each half of the binary structure into a slow part (labeled **a** in the diagram below) and a fast part (**b**). In the Larghetto (a setting of lines 1–4), Serpina addresses Uberto with mock melancholy and tells him what he will say when, in the future, he thinks of her. In the Allegro (lines 5–6), she reveals her real feelings to the audience.

**Parallel binary form in the A section**

| FORM | First Part | | | | Second Part | | |
|---|---|---|---|---|---|---|---|
| | Rit. 1 | **a** | **b** | Rit. 2 | **a'** | **b'** | Rit. 3 |
| KEY (I = B♭) | I | I–V | V | V | V–I | I | I |
| TEMPO | Adagio | | Allegro | | Adagio | Allegro | |
| TEXT (LINES) | | 1–4 | 5–6 | | 1–4 | 5–6 | |
| MEASURES | 1–3 | 3–10 | 11–26 | 26–30 | 30–36 | 37–52 | 52–60 |

Pergolesi similarly divided the **B** section into a Larghetto (a setting of lines 7–9) and an Allegro (lines 10–11), both in G minor, differentiating Serpina's (insincere) apology to Uberto for behaving badly from another cheerful aside to the audience.

In Serpina's music, whether addressed to Uberto or to the audience, Pergolesi used galant mannerisms selectively to emphasize the contrasting character of her impersonations. In the opening melody, the appoggiaturas in measure 6 have something of the same effect—an expression of tender melancholy—as those at the beginning of Hasse's *Per questo dolce amplesso* (see Anthology 3). But by dwelling on augmented-sixth harmony in measures 6–7, Pergolesi imbued Uberto's future words with pathos so exaggerated as to be comic. Serpina sings a Prinner (a voice-leading schema that, as explained in Chapter 3 of *Music in the Eighteenth Century*, involves a $\hat{6}$–$\hat{5}$–$\hat{4}$–$\hat{3}$ descent in the treble over a $\hat{4}$–$\hat{3}$–$\hat{2}$–$\hat{1}$ descent in the bass) in both the first Larghetto (m. 5) and the first Allegro (mm. 15–18). In the Larghetto it contributes to the tone of (false) nostalgia, while in the Allegro dissonances on the downbeats give this passage a tartness in keeping with the real character of Serpina, whose name means "little snake." These dissonances are like harmless little snakebites.

In weaving the three characters that Serpina portrays in *A Serpina penserete* into an aria in da capo form, Pergolesi and Federico exemplified one of the great achievements of eighteenth-century music: the expression of contrasting moods, personalities, and dramatic situations within single movements (instrumental as well as vocal) that retain their structural integrity despite their internal variety.

## Artaserse: Per questo dolce amplesso
### 1730

From *The Favourite Songs in the Opera Call'd Artaxerxes* by Sig. Hasse (London: John Walsh, 1734). Courtesy of Daniel Heartz.

Per questo dolce amplesso,
Per questo estremo addio,
Serbami o padre mio
L'idolo amato.

Sol questo all'ombra mia
Pace e conforto sia
Nel fier mio fato.

*Through this sweet embrace,*
*through this final farewell,*
*save, oh father,*
*my beloved.*

*Only this can give my ghost*
*peace and comfort,*
*in the midst of my cruel fate.*

The great male soprano Carlo Broschi (known as Farinelli) created the role of Arbace in Johann Adolf Hasse's setting of Pietro Metastasio's libretto *Artaserse* (Artaxerxes; Venice, 1730). Hasse, fresh from several years of study and practice in Naples, wrote for Farinelli this exquisite aria in E major, the text of which is not actually by Metastasio, but was inserted into the libretto by a local poet in preparation for Hasse's setting.

Arbace, unjustly accused of regicide, is about to face what he believes to be certain death. He bids farewell to his father and asks him to take care of his beloved Mandane. The situation is tragic, yet the young hero manages to keep his emotions under control. The text expresses tender melancholy rather than intense sorrow or anger. Hasse's music embodies, above all, qualities associated with the text's first adjective, "dolce" (sweet).

Farinelli, following a widespread eighteenth-century practice, brought *Per questo dolce amplesso* with him when he left Venice and continued to win applause with it in other cities. A publisher in London issued an edition of Hasse's aria in 1734–35 as a souvenir of Farinelli's performance of it in England; we reprint it here, with measure numbers added.

Notice that the edition mentions the singer, but not the composer, indicative of how closely singers were identified with the music written for them. It serves as a reminder that the score is but a framework for a performance that involved elaborate vocal improvisation. Farinelli's audience heard something different every time they went to the theater; this helps to explain the practice, common in the eighteenth century, of audience members returning repeatedly to the theater during an opera's run. The written (or in this case printed) score can give us only a very incomplete picture of what the audience in Venice—or later in London—actually heard on any one night.

We can nevertheless derive from the score solid information about general outlines of Hasse's aria. It is in dal segno form: the opening **A** section is repeated after the **B** section. But the second **A** is shorter than the first; it begins at measure 7, which is marked with a sign (*segno*) that resembles a capital S. At the end of **B**, Hasse probably wrote "Dal segno al fine" (from the sign to the end), but the English publisher garbled this to "Da Capo al Segno" (from the top to the sign), which makes no sense. (Primary sources like this early print are the best sources we have for eighteenth-century music, but we should keep in mind that those who produced them sometimes made mistakes.) Hasse signaled the end of the aria (which coincides with the end of **A**) with a fermata at measure 32.

**Large-scale form**

| FORM | A | B | A' |
|---|---|---|---|
| KEY (I = E) | I | IV–I | I |
| TEXT (LINES) | 1–4 | 5–7 | 1–4 |
| MEASURES | 1–32 | 33–44 | 71–32 |

As is normal with da capo and dal segno arias, the **A** section is in parallel binary form, with each part of the binary structure a setting of the first stanza of the aria text. (Taking into account the repetition of **A**, Farinelli sang the text of the first stanza four times.) After a six-measure orchestral introduction, the first part modulates to the dominant, B major, and cadences there. The second part begins with some tonal instability but soon returns to the tonic and ends with a four-measure ritornello. The **B** section, a setting of the second stanza, is in the subdominant (A major), a tonal area the **A** section left unexplored. The short ritornello at the end of **B**, by returning to the opening melody and the key of the **A** section, serves as a transition back to the beginning of **A**'s vocal line (thus allowing the orchestra to skip **A**'s first ritornello when it plays **A** a second time).

**Parallel binary form in the A section**

| FORM | | | First part | | Second part | |
|---|---|---|---|---|---|---|
| | Rit. 1 | a | | Rit. 2 | a' | Rit. 3 |
| KEY (I = E) | I | I–V | | V | /\/\/\I | I |
| TEXT (LINES) | | 1–4 | | | 1–4 | |
| MEASURES | 1–6 | 7–16 | | 16–17 | 18–29 | 29–32 |

In keeping with the keyword "dolce," the major mode prevails throughout, with the exception of measure 18, where a momentary tonicization of F♯ minor and a melodic leap of a diminished seventh hint at Arbace's distress. The sense of relaxation conveyed by the move to the subdominant at the beginning of the **B** section nicely underlines the meaning of the phrase "pace e conforto" (peace and comfort).

Balanced phrases unfold over a relatively slow-moving bass line to which repeated notes give rhythmic impetus. Lombard rhythms (reversed dotted rhythms) and three-note slides enliven the melody and suggest, perhaps, sobs. The opening melody elaborates an ascent from scale degree $\hat{1}$ up to $\hat{3}$ over I–V–I harmony. This is a common pattern in galant music; but Hasse skillfully manipulated it, using appoggiaturas (often equated with sighs in the eighteenth century) to emphasize the crucial words "amplesso" (embrace) and "addio" (farewell). The poem's first stanza ends with the words "l'idolo amato" (my beloved); the accented second syllable of the last word invited Hasse and Farinelli to create coloratura passages at the end of **A** and **A'**, which they did.

## 4

LODOVICO GIUSTINI (1685–1743)

# Piano Sonata No. 1 in G Minor: Movement 2
## Published 1732

Edited by John A. Rice. Source: *Sonata da cimbalo di piano e forte, detto volgarmente di martelletti* (Florence, 1732).

Lodovico Giustini, an exact contemporary of George Frideric Handel, Johann Sebastian Bach, and Domenico Scarlatti, belonged to the avant garde of his day in his exploitation of the piano and its potential for dynamic contrast. The piano was only about 30 years old when Giustini published his 12 sonatas—the first explicitly intended for the new instrument—in Florence, the city where Bartolomeo Cristofori had invented it. Giustini's title page shows that the invention was still causing terminological difficulties; he referred to the instrument with the clumsy phrase "cimbalo di piano e forte detto volgarmente di martelletti" (keyboard instrument with soft and loud, commonly called [keyboard instrument] with little hammers).

Giustini's sonatas consist of four or five movements, labeled both with the titles of seventeenth-century dances and with more modern tempo designations. The opening sonata, in G minor, has five movements: Balletto (Spiritoso, ma non presto), Corrente (Allegro), Sarabanda (Grave), Giga (Presto), and Minuet.

The Italian seventeenth-century *corrente* and the French *courante* were both dances in triple meter. Giustini, in giving the title *Corrente* to this duple-meter movement, was perhaps thinking of the literal meaning of the word *corrente* (running). This fast movement is in parallel binary form, which Giustini used as a framework for a series of contrasting musical ideas.

| FORM | First Part | Second Part |
|---|---|---|
| | ⫶A⫶ | ⫶A'⫶ |
| KEY (i = G MINOR) | i–III | III–i |
| MEASURE | 1–29 | 30–64 |

The first part of the binary structure begins with a six-measure melody in the form **ABB'**, fashionable in the opera arias of Giustini's younger contemporaries such as Johann Adolf Hasse, who often set the first line of an aria text once, as phrase **A**, and the second line twice, as phrase **B**. The modulatory passage that follows (mm. 7–14) leads to the relative major and a new melodic idea (mm. 15–22), which is followed by closing material (mm. 23–29).

The second part of the movement, slightly longer than the first, begins with a two-measure idea derived from the first theme, but now in the relative major. An area of tonal instability leads quickly to a return to the tonic, whose dominant, D major, is reached by means of what Robert Gjerdingen calls a "converging cadence": a typically galant half cadence in which the bass moves chromatically from the fourth scale degree up to the fifth—here, C–C♯–D (mm. 34–35). The second part ends with closing material identical to that in the first part, except that now, of course, it is in G minor.

Giustini took care not to exceed the capabilities of Cristofori's pianos. The Corrente has a range of three octaves and a minor seventh, from *D* up to *c'''*, which fits perfectly within the four-octave range of two surviving Cristofori instruments (*C* up to *c'''*). Giustini called attention to the **ABB'** form of the opening melody by directing that phrase **B'** be played quietly; he asked for a similar echo effect in the melody in B♭ major. He enhanced the energy and emphasis of cadences by marking the most important ones (at the end of both parts) *forte*.

These cadences use a pattern in the bass (scale degrees $\hat{3}$–$\hat{4}$–$\hat{5}$–$\hat{6}$, $\hat{3}$–$\hat{4}$–$\hat{5}$–$\hat{1}$) that was common in vocal music by younger opera composers of the 1720s and 1730s. But Giustini's reliance on this and other devices characteristic of vocal music does not mean that he wrote unidiomatically for the keyboard. Over this conventional bass he placed sixteenth-note passagework for the right hand calculated for its brilliant effect on the piano.

## 5

# DOMENICO SCARLATTI (1685–1757)

## Sonata in C Major, K. 421

### 1753 or earlier

Edited by John A. Rice. Source: Parma, Conservatorio Boito, Manuscript AG 3106–31420, vol. 8 (dated 1753).

1. In the manuscript source, measure 46 is the same as measure 38; following the analogous passage in the second part (mm. 121–122 in this edition), I have omitted the source's measure 46.

2. Scarlatti occasionally used the letter *M* to indicate notes in the upper staff that are to be played with the left hand.

Domenico Scarlatti spent much of his early career as a music director, composing and conducting church music in Rome and Lisbon (where, in addition to his more public duties, he served as keyboard instructor to the daughter of the king of Portugal). But when he went to Spain in 1729, as Princess Maria Barbara's personal musician, his professional activity was largely restricted to the composition and performance of keyboard music. For Maria Barbara, who eventually became queen of Spain, he wrote most of his 555 surviving keyboard sonatas. He found in the one-movement, binary-form sonata the ideal vehicle for the expression of his artistic personality, creating an oeuvre that, in its size, originality, and beauty, constitutes one of the greatest achievements in the history of keyboard music.

Scarlatti's Sonata in C Major, K. 421, is in parallel binary form, with repeats. It consists of two parts, the first modulating from tonic C to dominant G, the second (nine measures longer) modulating from G minor back to C. Using the same basic structure as Giustini's Corrente (see Anthology 4), Scarlatti composed his movement on a much larger scale: at 142 measures, it is more than twice as long as Giustini's. (Of course, the Corrente was only one of five movements in Giustini's Sonata in G Minor.) Each of Scarlatti's binary parts falls into two subsections (**a** and **b** in the diagram below) separated by a measure of silence prolonged by a fermata. The first subsection ends with a half cadence; the second with a full cadence.

| FORM | First Part | | Second Part | |
|---|---|---|---|---|
| | ‖:A:‖ | | ‖:A′:‖ | |
| | **a** | **b** | **a′** | **b′** |
| KEY (I = C) | I /\/\/\/\ | V | v /\/\/\/\ | I |
| MEASURES | 1–29 | 31–66 | 67–105 | 107–142 |

The first part begins with a call to attention in octaves: an ascending triadic zigzag. But aside from this striking and memorable opening gesture (much altered when it reappears at the beginning of the second part), this movement is a study in repeated sixteenth notes. The piquant dissonances of C♯ against B♭ and F♮ (mm. 9–12), as part of a sudden tonicization of D minor, give us a sample of Scarlatti's eccentric harmonic taste. They launch a modulatory passage that ends more conventionally, with a half cadence (V of V, at m. 29) approached by a Fonte (the two-step, minor–major descending sequence of which we have already seen an example in the opening duet of Pergolesi's *Stabat Mater*, Anthology 1, mm. 18–21). The Fonte here tonicizes first A minor, then G major, the dominant (mm. 17–24; this was a common way for galant composers to modulate to the dominant in the first part of binary movements). The rest of the first part (subsection **b**), in the dominant, consists of three drives to full cadences, each played twice.

One might suppose that six phrases all ending with full cadences in G major would annoy the player and the listener, especially when the same phrases return, transposed to the tonic, at the end of the second part of the binary structure (subsection **b'**). But anyone who feels that way is not familiar with Scarlatti's astonishing melodic and harmonic creativity.

Each pair of cadential phrases involves a different pattern of repeated notes, and all of them contain something that keeps them from sounding like the formulas to which composers of every age tend to gravitate at cadences. Most remarkable is the sense of rising excitement that comes from progressively shorter phrases and increasing overlap between the end of one phrase and the beginning of the next. The first cadential phrase is eight measures long (mm. 31–38), and together with its repetition it constitutes a conventional 16-measure period (mm. 31–46). The second phrase is only seven measures long, and its repetition begins at the same time as the first statement ends, resulting in an overall length of 13 measures (mm. 46–58). The third and final cadential idea (mm. 58–66) is the shortest of all: a nine-measure period consisting of two overlapping five-measure phrases, which gain charm by presenting one sequence of notes (marked with brackets in the example below) in two different harmonic and metric contexts. Scarlatti loved the repeated cadences of the galant style because, paradoxically, they offered him the opportunity for limitless invention.

## 6

JOSEPH BOULOGNE, CHEVALIER DE

SAINT-GEORGES (1745–1799)

# Violin Concerto in D Major, Op. 3, No. 1: Movement 2
## Published 1773

Piano reduction by John A. Rice. Based on full score edited by Allan Badley (Wellington: Artaria Editions, 2002).

Strings

Violins without mutes

arco

cresc.

Full orchestra          Strings (violins with mutes)

+ Flutes          + Horns

Son of a French colonial official and an African slave on the island of Guadeloupe, the Chevalier de Saint-Georges came to France with his father, who gave him a good education and training in fencing and music. He excelled in both, becoming one of France's best violinists and a distinguished composer.

Saint-Georges may have studied composition with François-Joseph Gossec, France's leading composer of symphonies. Eighteenth-century instrumental virtuosos frequently wrote concertos for their own use in concerts; it was thus to this genre, rather than to the symphony, that Saint-Georges directed most of his creative energy. His relations with Gossec gave him access to the Concert des Amateurs, an orchestra that Gossec founded in 1769. The several violin concertos published by Saint-Georges during the 1770s, including the Violin Concerto in D Major, Op. 3, No. 1, were probably first played by the composer himself during concerts given by the Concert des Amateurs.

After the festive sounds of the concerto's first movement in D major, full of exuberant virtuosity, the Adagio in D minor presents an entirely different emotional world. Saint-Georges reinforced the effect of the new tempo and mode by silencing the oboes that contribute to the warmth and brilliance of the first movement's sonorities. Only pairs of flutes and horns accompany the strings (the violins with mutes) in the slow movement.

The Adagio uses binary form without repeats. Much like the **A** section of a da capo aria, it extends binary form by adding three orchestral ritornellos: before, between, and after the two solo passages:

| FORM | First Part | | | Second Part | |
|---|---|---|---|---|---|
| | Rit. 1 | Solo 1 | Rit. 2 | Solo 2 | Rit. 3 |
| KEY (i = D MINOR) | i | i–III | III | III–i | i |
| MEASURES | 1–8 | 9–28 | 28–32 | 33–51 | 51–61 |

In the first ritornello (or orchestral introduction), the violas play a ghostly repeated A above the violins; these repeated eighth notes return, twice, later in the movement. Entering at measure 9, the soloist, spinning a simple yet eloquent line, conveys a sense of loneliness and desolation. Although the modulatory passage that begins at measure 16 plunges directly into the relative major, F, the new key is not fully confirmed until the converging cadence at measures 19–20 causes us to hear C as the dominant. The second melodic area (mm. 21–28) begins with a short canon accompanied by the repeated eighth notes from the beginning of the movement.

The second part of the binary structure begins in F major, but soon returns to the darkness of the minor mode. As both soloist and composer, Saint-Georges used the expressive melodic interval of the diminished seventh (mm. 38–40) to convey a sense of pain and sorrow. But just as effective was his decision to bring back the canonic passage heard earlier in F major, now in D minor and more richly orchestrated (mm. 44–47)—a strategy that Mozart was to use often in minor-mode movements, with equally moving results.

## 7

DOMENICO GALLO (DATES UNKNOWN)

# Trio Sonata No. 1 in G Major: Movement 1
## 1750–1760?

Edited by John A. Rice. Source: *Twelve Sonatas for Two Violins and a Bass or an Orchestra compos'd by Gio. Batt.ª Pergolese, author of the Stabat Mater* (London, 1780).

In 1780 a music publisher in London issued a set of trio sonatas under the title *Twelve Sonatas for Two Violins and a Bass or an Orchestra compos'd by Gio. Batt.ª Pergolese*. According to a note on the title page, a gentleman on the Grand Tour had found the sonatas in a manuscript in Italy. Like many tourists, he brought the music back to England with him—one of the ways in which the Grand Tour enriched musical life in Britain. Whether the manuscript's title page or the English publisher first attributed the sonatas to Giovanni Battista Pergolesi we do not know; nor do we know if the attribution was an honest mistake or a deliberate falsification, taking advantage of the extraordinary prestige that Pergolesi had won with such works as the *Stabat Mater* and *La serva padrona* (Anthology 1 and 2). In any case, Pergolesi certainly did not write these trio sonatas, which are now attributed to the little-known Domenico Gallo.

Trio Sonata No. 1 in G Major combines elements of the galant and learned, with an emphasis on the latter. Its publication in London in the late eighteenth century serves as a useful reminder of the continued popularity, at least in some parts of Europe, of genres and compositional techniques associated with the seventeenth century.

The delicate and ebullient first movement is in binary form, without repeats. The second part (mm. 15–42) is exactly twice as long as the first. In this respect this movement differs greatly from the binary movements (vocal as well as instrumental) we have considered so far, in which the second part is only moderately longer than the first part.

| FORM | First Part | Second Part | |
|---|---|---|---|
| | A | B | A′ |
| KEY (I = G) | I–V | V–iii /\/\/\ | I |
| MEASURE | 1–14 | 15–30 | 31–42 |

The second part begins with a statement of the first theme in the dominant, then moves from the dominant to its relative minor (B) before tracing its way back to the tonic by means of two successive Fontes (two-step descending sequences at mm. 27–30). The return of the tonic (at m. 31) coincides with a restatement of the movement's opening theme. This "double return" is a characteristic element of rounded binary form; we will see it in many other movements in this anthology. The content of the rest of the movement closely parallels that of the first part, except that it stays in the tonic. The absence of binary repeats in Gallo's movement and the division of the second part of the binary structure into two subsections, the second of which begins with a double return, make this a good example of a binary-form movement that simultaneously projects a ternary pattern (**ABA′**), even though in this case the middle section is melodically very similar to the first and third.

Gallo's Moderato opens with a pair of balanced two-measure phrases elaborating voice-leading schemata characteristic of the galant style. Both phrases begin with a romanesca, involving a bass line that descends stepwise from the tonic. In the first phrase the romanesca is followed by a Prinner, in which (as in the examples we have pointed to in Pergolesi's *A Serpina penserete*, Anthology 2, mm. 5 and 15–18) a melodic line descending through scale degrees $\hat{6}$–$\hat{5}$–$\hat{4}$–$\hat{3}$ is accompanied by a bass descending from $\hat{4}$ to $\hat{1}$. The second romanesca leads, in contrast, to a converging cadence: a half cadence in which the bass ascends chromatically, $\hat{4}$–$\sharp\hat{4}$–$\hat{5}$ (for another example, see Lodovico Giustini's Corrente, Anthology 4, mm. 34–35).

But the potentially galant effect of this music is undercut by the melodic independence of the second violin part, the actively moving bass line, and the fast harmonic rhythm. The movement unfolds without much dramatization of internal contrast. The modulation from G to D is so inconspicuous that listeners might be tempted to hear the first part of the binary structure as a ritornello of the kind that Vivaldi used at the beginning of many of his concerto movements (but such opening ritornellos usually stay in the tonic, or at least end there). All these aspects of the Trio Sonata No. 1 must have appealed to the British taste for "ancient music" when it was published in London in 1780. And yet the closing material (mm. 10–14 and 38–42), with its repeated cadences, speaks to a more modern taste. It helps to explain why this sonata was published under Pergolesi's name and why musicians from the eighteenth century to the twentieth (including Igor Stravinsky, who reused this music in his ballet *Pulcinella*) accepted the attribution.

## JOHANN CHRISTIAN BACH (1735–1782)

# Sonata in D Major, Op. 5, No. 2: Movement 1
### Published 1766

Edited by John A. Rice. Source: *Six Sonatas for the Piano Forte or Harpsichord*, Op. 5 (London, 1765).

In 1766 Johann Christian Bach issued his Opus 5, *Six Sonatas for the Piano Forte or Harpsichord.*
The order of instruments on the title page is significant, emphasizing that the primary instrument for which they were composed was the piano. The sonatas themselves, with a substantial
number of indications of dynamic contrast, confirm that Bach, one of the first professional musicians to play the piano in a public concert, intended these sonatas for the piano.

The second sonata in the set is in D major, a key that composers used very often for operatic
overtures (probably because the large number of open strings available to violinists in this
key and its dominant made their instruments sound especially vibrant and because trumpets
and drums were frequently tuned in D). The opening movement of this sonata conveys some
of the energy and excitement associated with the eighteenth-century overture.

This movement is in rounded binary form with a double return; moreover, in signaling
changes of musical function with changes of dynamics, texture, melodic style, and harmonic

rhythm, it exemplifies what in the nineteenth century came to be called sonata form. Using terminology associated with sonata form, we can call the first part of the binary structure the exposition, and the second part the development and recapitulation.

| FORM | First Part | Second Part | |
|---|---|---|---|
| | ‖Exposition‖ | ‖Development‖ | ‖Recapitulation‖ |
| KEY (I = D) | I–V | V ∧∧∧ | I |
| MEASURES | 1–42 | 43–72 | 73–111 |

The exposition begins with massive chords that resemble those that open many eighteenth-century symphonies, such as Johann Stamitz's Symphony in D Major (Anthology 12). A two-measure *piano* response follows the two-measure *forte* opening. Then, moving from one level of balanced phrases to another, a repetition of the four-measure unit completes the first theme (mm. 1–9), which perfectly fulfills its multiple functions of attracting the listener's attention, communicating a sense of splendor and excitement, and asserting as strongly as possible the role of D major as home key.

The passage that follows (mm. 9–18) has a transitional, modulatory function. It offers contrast not only in its tonal instability, but also in its new texture—weaving sixteenth notes in the right hand approximate the effect of string tremolos—and its steady *forte* dynamic. It establishes a new key—the dominant, A major—by reaching a half cadence on its dominant. A second tonally stable area begins with a new theme (mm. 19–34), the movement's most lyrical music. The exposition ends with cadential material, whose *piano – forte* contrast played out in two-measure blocks recalls the dynamic contrast of the opening theme and reverses it.

## Exposition

| FORM | Melodic area 1 | Modulatory passage | Melodic area 2 | Closing material |
|---|---|---|---|---|
| KEY (I = D) | I | I–V/V | V | V |
| MEASURES | 1–9 | 9–18 | 19–34 | 35–42 |

The development presents, after a brief statement of the dominant, an area of tonal instability that uses various motives heard in the first part (with the conspicuous exception of the opening theme) and leads to a cadence in B minor. But the ultimate goal is the double return: the simultaneous return to tonic D major and the movement's opening chords, which occurs, after an eight-measure dominant pedal, at measure 73.

The rest of the movement consists of a restatement (or recapitulation) of material from the first part, but rearranged so that the connecting material stays in the tonic, while the second melodic area and the cadential area, previously in A, are now heard in D. Bach enhanced the effect of the new tonal context by shifts of register. He presented the first four-measure phrase a fourth higher than it sounded in the exposition, then shifted down an octave for the second phrase. To bring the movement to a suitably brilliant close, most of the closing material sounds a fourth higher than at the end of the exposition.

## 9

# CHRISTOPH GLUCK (1714–1787)

## *Orfeo ed Euridice*: Act 2, Scene 1, to end of chorus *Misero giovane*

### 1762

**Maestoso**

Orchestra I: strings, oboes, horns

Edited by John A. Rice. Principal source: Full score, ed. Hermann Albert, in *Denkmäler der Tonkunst in Österreich*, vol. 44a (Vienna, 1914), 50–64.

Orchestra II: harp, strings

## Coro

**Marcato, andante un poco**

Chi    mai dell' E - re-bo   fra le ca - li - gi-ni sull' or - me

Orchestra I

d'Er - co-le   e   di   Pi - ri - to - o   con - du - ce il   piè?

## Ballo

## Coro

Chi    mai dell' E – re-bo    fra le ca – li – gi – ni  sull' or – me  d'Er – co – le

Orchestra I

E lo spa - ven - - - ti - no gli ur - li di

Cer - be - ro, se un dio non è!

D'or - ror l'in - gom - bri - no

le fie - re Eu - me - ni - di   e   lo  spa - ven - - ti - no

gli ur - li  di  Cer - be - ro,  se un  dio  non  è!

Segue il Ballo, girando intorno ad Orfeo per spaventarlo.

Orfeo

Deh pla-

Orchestra II: strings, harp

**Coro**

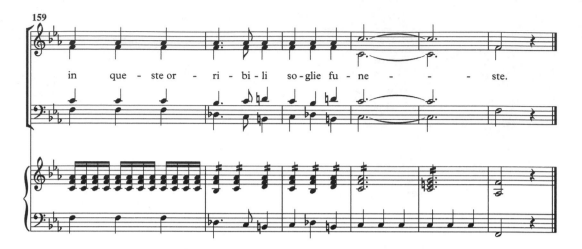

in que - ste or - ri - bi - li so - glie fu - ne - - ste.

CHORUS

| Chi mai dell'Erebo | *Who approaches through* |
| Fra le caligini | *the mists of Erebus,* |
| Sull'orme d'Ercole | *in the footsteps of Hercules* |
| E di Piritoo | *and of Pirithous?* |
| Conduce il piè? | |
| D'orror l'ingrombrino | *May the fierce Eumenides* |
| Le fiere Eumenidi | *obstruct him* |
| E lo spaventino | *and may he be terrified* |
| Gli urli di Cerbero, | *by the shrieks of Cerberus,* |
| Se un dio non è! | *unless he is god!* |

ORFEO

Deh placatevi con me,            *Please calm yourselves for me,*
Furie, larve, ombre sdegnose!    *Furies, ghosts, angry shades!*

CHORUS

No!            *No!*

ORFEO

Vi renda almen pietose       *Show some pity, at least,*
Il mio barbaro dolor!        *for my cruel sadness.*

CHORUS

No!                                            *No!*

CHORUS

Misero giovane,                                *Poor young man,*
Che vuoi, che mediti?                          *what do you want? What is your plan?*
Altro non abita                                *There is nothing*
Che lutto e gemito                             *but grief and weeping*
In queste orribili                             *in these horrible,*
Soglie funeste.                                *funereal dwellings.*

*Orfeo ed Euridice* (Orpheus and Eurydice), first performed in Vienna's Burgtheater on October 5, 1762, in celebration of the name day of Emperor Francis I, is not a full-length opera but a *festa teatrale*: a relatively short musical drama that often involves dance and chorus. The brevity of the *festa teatrale* and its associations with theatrical elements other than solo song encouraged Christoph Gluck and his collaborators (the poet Ranieri de Calzabigi, the choreographer Gasparo Angiolini, and the male soprano Gaetano Guadagni) to treat the opera as a demonstration of what could be achieved by the synthesis of Italian singing, pantomime ballet, and chorus that such theorists as Francesco Algarotti had been promoting during the 1750s.

In Act 2 of Gluck's opera, Orfeo (the musician Orpheus of Greek mythology, a role created by Guadagni), having descended to the underworld in search of his dead wife Euridice (Eurydice), finds his way blocked by the Furies and ghosts. Their confrontation is played out musically in a series of closely integrated passages for the vocal soloist, orchestra, chorus, and dancers.

Calzabigi gave the following directions for staging this scene: "As soon as the scene opens, to the sound of terrifying instrumental music [*orribile sinfonia*] the dance of the Furies and ghosts begins. It is interrupted by the harmony of Orfeo's lyre. When he appears on the stage, the whole infernal crowd sings the following chorus." Gluck's music corresponds exactly to this scenario. The "terrifying instrumental music" is a 20-measure, tonally unstable Maestoso characterized by the interval of the diminished seventh, melodic as well as harmonic. A rising sequence progressively intensifies the emotional pitch, which reaches its climax in a descending chain of suspensions over a dominant pedal (mm. 13–15).

| | Dance of Furies and ghosts | Orfeo enters | Chorus of Furies | Dance | Chorus of Furies | Repetition of one of the previous dances | Orfeo's solo | Chorus of Furies |
|---|---|---|---|---|---|---|---|---|
| **TEMPO** | Maestoso | [no tempo] | Marcato, andante un poco | Presto | Andante | Maestoso or Presto | [Andante] | Andante |
| **METER** | ¢ | c | $\frac{3}{4}$ | $\frac{3}{4}$ | $\frac{3}{4}$ | ¢ or $\frac{3}{4}$ | c | $\frac{3}{4}$ |
| **KEY** | E♭ | C minor | C minor | C minor | C minor | E♭ or C minor | E♭ | E♭ minor–F minor |
| **TEXT (LINES)** | | 1–5 | | 1–10 | | | 11–16 | 17–22 |
| **MEASURES** | 1–20 | 21–23 | 24–33 | 34–50 | 51–90 | 1–20 or 34–50 | 91–132 | 133–164 |

Orfeo announces his arrival with the sound of a harp accompanied by an orchestra of strings playing pizzicato. He has little time to appear on stage, and no time at all to sing, because after only three measures of harp, the chorus interrupts to confront the intruder. First the Furies and ghosts hurl stark unisons at Orfeo; then, after a violent dance (Presto), they intensify their hostility with diminished seventh chords. At the words "gli urli di Cerbero" (the shrieks of Cerberus), three rapid scales in the orchestra depict the barking of the three-headed dog that guards the underworld.

At this point Calzabigi's libretto contains the instructions "The dance follows, circling around Orfeo to frighten him." Although this leaves in doubt which of the two previously performed dances ought to be repeated here, most recent productions (and recordings) repeat the opening Maestoso.

Unintimidated by this awesome display of supernatural power, Orfeo uses his harp to steer the tonality from C minor to E♭ major (mm. 91–93). He makes his first attempt to tame the Furies, singing "Deh placatevi con me" (Please calm yourselves for me) to a sweet melody in E♭, and in the parallel binary form that Gluck, like other opera composers, used in the **A** sections of da capo arias. The Furies and ghosts interrupt with shouts of "No!" but allow Orfeo to finish his plea; evidently his words and music have already begun to work their magic.

*Deh placatevi con me*: **binary structure**

| FORM | First Part | Second Part |
|---|---|---|
| **KEY (I = E♭)** | I–V | i–I |
| **TEXT (LINES)** | 11–16 | 11–16 |
| **MEASURES** | 91–109 | 110–132 |

The full cadence at the end of "Deh placatevi" is, within the tonally fluid context of this scene, a major musical event, communicating the power of Orfeo's musicianship and eloquence. In the following chorus, "Misero giovane," the furies' hostility gives way to pity and curiosity, as they ask Orfeo what he seeks in the underworld. The chorus begins in E♭ minor but ends in F minor. The furies' inability to maintain control of tonality—in contrast to Orfeo's steadfast attachment to E♭ major in his previous solo—shows that their resistance is weakening.

Throughout the scene Gluck manipulates all the musical elements at his disposal—melody, tempo, meter, dynamics, orchestral color, mode, key—to depict the confrontation and Orfeo's gradual success in persuading the Furies and ghosts to let him pass. This success is not given full musical realization until the beginning of the next scene, which presents a picture—musical as well as visual—of Elysium, the place where, according to Greek mythology, the heroic and the virtuous go after death. The sound of F major, flutes, and the gentle rhythm of a minuet reinforce a visual transformation that replaces the horrors of the Furies, as if by magic, with the peaceful beauty of the Elysian Fields.

As Wendy Heller describes in *Music in the Baroque*, at the end of the sixteenth century the Greek myth of Orpheus inspired poets and musicians to invent opera. A little more than a century and a half later the same myth inspired Gluck and his collaborators to put into practice what many artists and theorists had been preaching since 1750.

Ⓢ **Norton Opera Sampler video available**

## 10

JOHANN BAPTIST VANHAL (1739–1813)

# *Missa Pastoralis*: **Agnus Dei**

1782 or before

Piano–vocal score by John A. Rice. Based on the full score edited by Allan Badley (Wellington, New Zealand: Artaria Editions, 2000).

cem, pa — — cem, pa — cem, pa — — cem, pa — cem.

Do – na no – bis pa – cem, pa – cem, do – na no – bis

Agnus Dei, qui tollis peccata mundi,
    miserere nobis.
Agnus Dei, qui tollis peccata mundi,
    miserere nobis.
Agnus Dei, qui tollis peccata mundi,
    dona nobis pacem.

*Lamb of God, who take away the sins of the world,*
    *have mercy on us.*
*Lamb of God, who take away the sins of the world,*
    *have mercy on us.*
*Lamb of God, who take away the sins of the world,*
    *give us peace.*

Johann Baptist Vanhal, born a serf in a small village in Bohemia, took advantage of the excellent musical education offered in many of that kingdom's schools to became a prolific and accomplished composer. As a young man he bought his freedom, finished his education by visiting the great musical centers of Italy, and settled in Vienna, where he lived for the rest of his life. But he never forgot his Bohemian roots; indeed in compositions such as the *Missa pastoralis* (Pastoral Mass) he celebrated them.

The *Missa pastoralis* is one of many eighteenth-century works, instrumental as well as vocal, that incorporate tunes played by central European shepherds on rustic bagpipes or horns. (Although we now associate the bagpipe with Scotland and with soldiers and police, the eighteenth century associated it, and its distinctive drones, much more with shepherds and other country folk.) Because shepherds play an important role in the Christmas story, much pastoral music has to do with Christmas; and the link between pastoral music and the Nativity was especially strong in the rural churches of Vanhal's native land. Festively scored for two oboes, two trumpets in C, timpani, and strings, his *Missa pastoralis* makes use in every movement of drones and the triadic horn signals with which eighteenth-century shepherds and cowherds called their animals.

At the beginning of the Agnus Dei, the last movement, the oboes and trumpets are silent, and the musical references to the pastoral temporarily cease. Solemnity suddenly replaces the festivity that pervades most of this mass. G major, the key that has prevailed up to this point, gives way to the parallel minor. A lovely Adagio consists of three musical sections that correspond to the three parts of this prayer of supplication. The sections, progressively longer, start in one key and end in another: the first moves from G minor to its relative major, B♭, the second from B♭ major to D minor, and the third from D minor back to G minor (it ends on the dominant of G):

**Adagio**

| FORM | A | A′ | A″ |
|---|---|---|---|
| KEY (i = G MINOR) | i–III | III–v | v–i |
| TEXT (LINE) | 1 | 2 | 3 |
| MEASURES | 1–14 | 14–29 | 29–47 |

Vanhal, whose early Grand Tour of Italy brought him into intimate contact with the conventions of galant voice-leading, manipulated those conventions to dramatize the form of the Adagio. In the first section, what appears to be the beginning of a Prinner in G minor (E♭-D in the treble above C-B♭ in the bass) is interrupted by a cadence in the relative major. It is only in section 3 that the Prinner is allowed to reach completion (mm. 37–43): an effective way to confirm the return of the tonic key. The Adagio serves as a splendid slow introduction to the Allegro moderato with which the whole mass concludes.

With the Allegro moderato, the festive mood, major mode, and trumpets and timpani return, as do the pastoral melodic elements and drones. Taking up again the last three words of the Adagio, "dona nobis pacem" (give us peace), Vanhal set them to cheerful, folklike music in sonata form.

**Allegro moderato**

| FORM | First Part | Second Part | | Coda |
|---|---|---|---|---|
| | Exposition | Development | Recapitulation | |
| KEY (I = G MAJOR) | I–V | V | I | I |
| MEASURES | 48–90 | 91–98 | 99–132 | 132–163 |

The development gave composers an opportunity, even in predominantly bright movements, to explore darker, more complex, more mysterious parts of the musical and emotional spectrum. But Vanhal, having used the opening Adagio for precisely this kind of exploration, made the development as short as possible, and without any tonal instability or even so much as an allusion to the minor mode. As if to compensate for the brevity of the development, he added a long coda that brings the mass to a satisfying conclusion by returning to the pastoral horn signals and drones heard in earlier movements.

The combination of fast tempo, pervasive syncopations, major mode, and homophonic texture in Vanhal's concluding Allegro moderato may remind some listeners of another piece of eighteenth-century sacred music, *Inflammatus et accensus* in Giovanni Battista Pergolesi's *Stabat Mater* (1736; see Ex. 1.1 in *Music in the Eighteenth Century*). The classic status of Pergolesi's *Stabat Mater* (in Vienna as in the rest of Europe) made musical echoes of it inevitable. But the similarities between these works, composed as much as 45 years apart, attest to something more interesting than the possibility—even the likelihood—that Vanhal learned from Pergolesi. They remind us of the basically optimistic mind-set that characterized the Enlightenment and that affected religious ceremony as much as other aspects of life.

## 11

# CARL PHILIPP EMANUEL BACH (1714–1788)

# Fantasia in C Minor, Wq. 63/6, H. 75

## 1753

From *Carl Philipp Emanuel Bach: The Complete Works*, Series I, Volume 3 (Los Altos, CA: Packard Humanities Institute). Reprinted by permission of The Packard Humanities Institute.

Carl Philipp Emanuel Bach published this fantasy in his book *Versuch über die wahre Art das Clavier zu spielen* (Essay on the True Way of Playing the Keyboard, 1753–62), as one of 18 *Probestücke*, or trial pieces, illustrating points in the book. He referred to this particular piece in a passage that vividly conveys his aesthetic values: "It is primarily by means of fantasias, consisting not of previously memorized passages or borrowed ideas, but arising spontaneously from a good and musical soul, that the keyboard player—more than any other musician—can achieve the effect of speech, the abrupt surprise of changes in mood."

Bach went on to explain some distinctive aspects of the notation of fantasies:

> Common time is indicated, although not observed throughout—as is customary in this genre; for this reason bar-lines are always omitted in the fantasia. The duration of the notes is determined partly by the *moderato* indication, but mainly by the relative values of the notes themselves. Triplets can be identified wherever the notes are grouped in threes. Rhapsodic improvisation seems particularly appropriate for the expression of emotions, because every type of regular meter carries with it a certain constraint. Accompanied recitative illustrates well the way in which tempo and meter need to be changed frequently in order to arouse and to restrain many different emotions in rapid succession.

In mentioning accompanied recitative—vocal recitative accompanied by orchestra—Bach called attention to an ambition that shaped much of his instrumental music. Although he never wrote an opera, he composed for and improvised at the keyboard in such a way as to make the instrument sing, and in doing so to express the whole range of emotions represented on the operatic stage.

Use of the word *keyboard* here, instead of *harpsichord, piano,* or *clavichord,* takes account of the fact that the German word *Clavier* (or *Klavier*) can mean any of these instruments. But Bach was particularly fond of the clavichord, whose gentle sound and simple action allowed him, when he wanted, to hover poetically at the very edge of silence. The clavichord, moreover, offers one very "vocal" effect unattainable on either the harpsichord or the piano: by keeping the key in contact with a vibrating string and quickly varying the pressure of the finger, the player can produce a faintly perceptible vibrato that Bach referred to with the term *Bebung*.

The fantasy is in three parts: two improvisatory passages labeled Allegro moderato, without barlines, frame a lyrical Largo with barlines and in triple meter. The first unmeasured passage is about twice as long as the second. The piece begins and ends in C minor, but except for this tonal symmetry, the opening and closing sections are wildly unconventional in tonality, modulating freely and unexpectedly. Recitative-like passages in the right hand—a kind of nonverbal declamation—alternate with improvisatory runs that get faster as the fantasy unfolds.

| FORM | A | B | A′ |
|---|---|---|---|
| CHARACTER | Free fantasy; recitative | Minuet-like; galant | Free fantasy; recitative |
| KEY (i = C MINOR) | i ᘿᘿ | III ᘿᘿ | ᘿᘿ i |
| MEASURES | Unmeasured | 1–21 | Unmeasured |

The central Largo in E♭, in contrast, consists of a galant melody laid out, at least to begin with, in neat four-measure phrases, with parallel thirds in the right hand, repeated eighth notes in the accompaniment, and an orderly approach to the dominant that reaches V/V by means of a converging cadence (at mm. 7–8). The improvisatory, unconventional character of the opening unmeasured passage starts to infect the Largo after that: the four-measure phrases and parallel thirds are abandoned and the harmony becomes darker and more unstable. A return to E♭ and a cadence there (m. 15) marks the end of the Largo as a tonally closed melody. The rest of the music in triple meter consists of a transition to the second unmeasured passage.

The fantasy contains many sudden contrasts in dynamics. While such contrasts could be effectively realized on the eighteenth-century piano, Bach notated one dynamic effect with the clavichord in mind: single notes with four dots and a slur above them are to be played with vibrato (Bebung).

The fingerings in this edition are Bach's own, reflecting the pedagogical function of this piece within the *Versuch*.

C.P.E. Bach's works are traditionally referred to with two numbering systems. One, using the abbreviation Wq., is based on a catalogue by Alfred Wotquenne (1904); the other, using the abbreviation H., is based on a catalogue by Eugene Helm (1989).

## 12

# JOHANN STAMITZ (1717–1757)

# Symphony in D Major, Op. 3, No. 2: Movement 1
## 1750–54

From *Mannheim Symphonists: A Collection of Twenty-Four Orchestral Works.* Edited by Hugo Riemann (New York: Broude Brothers).

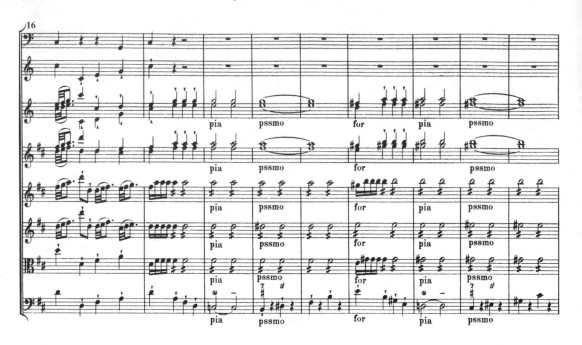

Under Elector Carl Theodor, the western German city of Mannheim became one of Europe's capitals of orchestral music in the mid-eighteenth century. The elector assembled excellent orchestral musicians and put in charge of them a young Bohemian composer and music director, Johann Stamitz, who melded them into the well-disciplined and powerful ensemble for which he wrote brilliant symphonies.

The "invention, fire and contrast" that Charles Burney praised in Stamitz's symphonic fast movements are easy to find in the opening Presto of this symphony in D major, in which Stamitz expanded parallel binary form by using it as a scaffold for the presentation of several passages that differ in function and style. Stamitz called for neither of the binary sections to be repeated; this helped him suffuse the movement with a pleasing sense of structural ambiguity.

Six massive chords, separated by rests, grab the audience's attention, display the orchestra's power and precision, and establish the key of D major as the movement's tonic. Listeners hearing this movement for the first time will assume that these chords belong to the first part of the binary structure; but when they discover that the chords never return later in the movement (except at the very end), they might reinterpret them as a kind of introduction, and hear the binary structure as beginning at measure 5 with one of Stamitz's favorite devices: a crescendo over a tonic pedal that he adopted from Italian opera overtures, especially those of Niccolò Jommelli. The crescendo culminates in a passage for full orchestra characterized by three-note slides (a galant mannerism we have already seen frequently in earlier Italian music, including the opening themes of Giovanni Battista Pergolesi's *A Serpina penserete* and Lodovico Giustini's Corrente; see Anthology 2 and 4) and a modulation to the dominant, A major: the key in which we hear the movement's only lyrical tune, *piano*, played by strings alone. The return of the full orchestra brings the first part of the binary structure, apparently, to a close.

We cannot be absolutely certain about the finality of this closure because Stamitz's decision not to repeat either part of the binary structure allowed him to elide the end of the first part with the beginning of the second part. The apparent end of the first part (at m. 53) is followed immediately by a repetition of the crescendo, now in the dominant. This crescendo serves as the beginning of the second part, but it can also be heard, in a kind of structural pun, as a continuation of the first part's closing material.

| FORM | Introduction | First part | | | Second part | | | Coda |
|---|---|---|---|---|---|---|---|---|
| CONTENT | Loud chords | Crescendo, modulation | Lyrical theme | Cadential material | Crescendo, modulation | Lyrical theme | Cadential material | Crescendo, loud chords |
| KEY (I = D) | I | I–V/V | V | V | V–V/I | I | I | I |
| MEASURES | 1–4 | 5–36 | 37–48 | 48–53 | 53–86 | 87–98 | 98–103 | 103–125 |

As the second part continues, it starts retracing the path taken earlier by the first, but now establishing A as the dominant, with a long pedal. The lyrical theme returns in the tonic. The closing material that follows constitutes the end of the second part. A third and final statement of the crescendo, now back in the tonic, serves as the first element of a short but thrilling coda.

In this Presto in D major, Stamitz called for two horns in D. The eighteenth-century horn was valveless and thus restricted in the number of pitches it could play without its hardware being altered. Hornists used crooks (interchangeable pieces of metal pipe of various lengths) to shorten or lengthen their instrument's tubing and thus increase the number of keys in which they could play. Stamitz's "horns in D" are horns with crooks that allow them to be conveniently played in D major. Their silence during the first statement of the lyrical theme provides welcome contrast, and helps to establish this theme as tonally removed from the movement's tonic. Conversely, when the lyrical theme returns later in the movement, the horns' participation in its performance (together with oboes) helps us hear the melody as being in the home key. Thus the horns contribute to the comprehensibility of Stamitz's tonal argument.

# 13

## ANNA BON (CA. 1740–?)

## Keyboard Sonata in F Major, Op. 2, No. 3: Movement 1
### 1757

Edited by John A. Rice. Source: *Sei sonate per il cembalo* (Nürnberg, 1757).

Anna Bon, the child of a professional singer (Rosa Ruvinetti) and a stage designer, librettist, and actor (Girolamo Bon), studied at one of Venice's conservatories for girls. When her parents established themselves at the court of Bayreuth under the patronage of the music-loving Margravine Wilhelmina, Anna joined them there, and with Wilhelmina's support she developed quickly into a skillful composer. She was only 17 years old when she published her *Sei sonate per il cembalo* (Six Keyboard Sonatas) in 1757, identifying herself on the title page as "Anna Bon di Venezia, virtuosa di musica di camera dell'Altezza Serenissima di Federico, Margravio Regnante di Brandenburg Culmbach" (Anna Bon of Venice, virtuoso in the chamber ensemble of Frederick, His Most Serene Highness, Margrave of Brandenburg-Culmbach). Frederick was Wilhelmina's husband; in referring to him as her employer, Bon was probably respecting Wilhelmina's desire to keep her musical activities and patronage private.

Bon's keyboard sonata uses the three-movement, fast-slow-fast format that Carl Philipp Emanuel Bach had adopted in his Prussian and Württemberg Sonatas of the early 1740s. In Bon's Sonata No. 3, an Allegretto and a Minuetto surround a central Adagio.

The Allegretto is in rounded binary form and begins, like Lodovico Giustini's Corrente (see Anthology 4), with a six-measure theme. Bon's texture rarely involves more than two parts: lean and transparent, it focuses the listener's attention on the beauty of a triplet-laden melodic line and on the miniature drama of contrasting ideas and changing keys that she presented on the binary stage. Unlike Giustini's sonatas and those of Bach's Prussian and

Württemberg sets, Bon supplied no dynamic indications, suggesting that the *cembalo* of her title page was primarily the harpsichord.

Bon's treatment of binary form resembles Domenico Gallo's (see Anthology 7) in her expansion of the second part, which is more than twice as long as the first; the double return (the simultaneous return of the tonic key and the opening melody, at m. 43, exactly halfway through the second part) would allow us to hear this movement, like Gallo's, as both binary and ternary were it not for the repeat signs with which Bon enclosed both parts of the binary structure.

| FORM | First Part | Second Part | |
|---|---|---|---|
| | ‖A‖ | ‖ B | A′ ‖ |
| KEY (I = F) | I–V | V–vi /\/\/\/\ | I |
| MEASURES | 1–20 | 21–42 | 43–66 |

## 14

JOSEPH HAYDN (1732–1809)

# Symphony No. 8 in G Major (*Le soir*): Movement 1
## 1761

From *Joseph Haydns Werke*, Series I, Volume 1 (Leipzig: Breitkopf und Härtel).

236

Among the stipulations to which Joseph Haydn agreed when he became director of the orchestra of Prince Paul Esterházy in 1761 was "to compose such music as His Serene Highness may command, and neither to communicate such compositions to any other person, nor to allow them to be copied, but he shall retain them for the exclusive use of His Highness, and not compose for any other person without the knowledge and gracious permission of His Highness." Thus it may have been on the prince's orders that shortly after Haydn signed this document he wrote three symphonies (No. 6, *Le matin*; No. 7, *Le midi*, and No. 8, *Le soir*) that depict the times of day: morning, noon, and evening.

The idea for such a project may have ultimately had literary inspiration. In 1756 the poet Friedrich Wilhelm Zachariae published *Die Tageszeiten* (The Times of Day), "a painterly poem" in four books: *Morning, Noon, Evening,* and *Night.* Although Haydn's scores make no explicit reference to Zachariae or his poem, the titles of the symphonies might have reminded German-reading audiences of the 1760s of Zachariae's *Tageszeiten.*

Historians of music have tended to celebrate the eighteenth century for its cultivation of abstract music—that is, music without any apparent pictorial or descriptive elements. Yet many listeners understood instrumental music as anything but abstract; instead they heard a series of contrasting musical elements—various combinations of rhythm, meter, key, melody, harmony, and tempo—that carried associations from opera, church music, dance, and the natural world. Haydn's *Le matin*, *Le midi*, and *Le soir* are among the hundreds of instrumental works that used such elements, which musicologists sometimes call "topics," to tell a story or to depict emotions, persons, or events. Eighteenth-century musicians described such works as "characteristic"; the term "program music" came into use only in the nineteenth century.

The first movement of *Le soir* has no title, but an appropriate one might be "A Night at the Opera in Vienna." Daniel Heartz's discovery that Haydn borrowed Christoph Gluck's song *Je n'aimais pas le tabac beaucoup* (I did not like tobacco much) for the main thematic material of this movement sheds light not only on the meaning of this symphony but also on Haydn's musical environment during the early years of his employment by the Esterházy princes. It reminds us that the Esterházy palace at Eisenstadt, where Haydn spent much of the year, was only a day's travel from Vienna.

Gluck's song had contributed to the success of his arrangement of the opéra comique *Le diable à quatre*, first performed in Vienna in 1759 and revived in 1761, the year of Haydn's symphony. In it, Margot explains that she started to enjoy snuff (powdered tobacco inhaled through the nose) only when her husband forbade her from taking it. The excitement of doing something forbidden now enhances her pleasure. Gluck's music conveys the playful, cheeky character of Margot's words. The accompaniment consists entirely of pizzicato strings. At the line "Mais mon mari me défend cela" (But my husband put it completely off limits), Margot impersonates her husband by singing in a low register. Gluck responded alertly and amusingly to the text's switch from nine- to six-syllable lines by shifting from four-measure phrases to a pert two-measure phrase, completely different in character from the rest of the melody, for the crucial words "depuis ce moment-là" (since that very moment). Gluck's song was a hit, published soon after the Viennese premiere and sung often in private concerts.

Christoph Gluck, *Je n'aimais pas le tabac beaucoup.* Source: Manuscript keyboard–vocal score (two staves only) from the archive of the Schwarzenberg family, Český Krumlov, Czech Republic.

*I did not like tobacco much; I took only a little, often none at all. But my husband put it completely off limits. From that time I have found it amusing to take it when I'm all alone, for it gets rid of boredom, whatever my husband says.*

Haydn's use of Gluck's song dramatizes the difference, in a large-scale binary-form movement like this one, between melodic, modulating, and closing material. Haydn differentiated these just as sharply here as Johann Christian Bach did in the first movement of his Sonata in D Major (see Anthology 8); the terminology of sonata form can be applied to this movement as usefully as to Bach's.

| FORM | First Part | Second Part | |
|---|---|---|---|
| | ‖A ‖ | ‖ B | A' ‖ |
| | Exposition | Development | Recapitulation |
| KEY (I = G) | I–V | V 〰〰 | I |
| MEASURES | 1–93 | 94–172 | 173–247 |

*Je n'aimais pas le tabac beaucoup* (transposed, reorchestrated, and with a few melodic details altered) serves as the first theme. The beginning of the connecting passage that follows (m. 34) is precisely the moment where Haydn stopped quoting and began composing.

**Detailed diagram of first part (exposition)**

| CONTENT | Melodic area 1 | Modulatory passage | Melodic area 2 | Closing material |
|---|---|---|---|---|
| AUTHORSHIP | Gluck | Haydn | Gluck and Haydn | Haydn |
| KEY (I = G) | I | I–V | V | V |
| MEASURES | 1–34 | 34–50 | 51–65 | 65–93 |

This does not mean he stopped using Gluck's music, which pervades the entire movement. Throughout his career Haydn enjoyed the compositional challenge of thematic economy: he demonstrated the musical satisfaction and intellectual stimulation of deriving entire movements from a small amount of melodic material. Gluck's authorship of that material makes Haydn's compositional achievement no less admirable. Nor does it keep us from being able to follow the clear distinction that Haydn, like most other composers of his time, made between melodic material (in this case mostly by Gluck) and modulatory and closing material (mostly by Haydn).

This movement contains evidence of Haydn's ambition, as recently appointed leader of the Esterházy orchestra, to challenge and please the players under his supervision with attractive solos. In the opening melodic section he embroidered Gluck's melody with little phrases for the flute (mm. 17–19 and 21–23). After the expected modulation to the dominant, a second melodic area begins with another quotation from Gluck, but this time assigned to two oboes (mm. 51–58). Near the beginning of the development, the flute has solo passagework worthy of a concerto (mm. 107–113). The double return that signals the beginning of the recapitulation (m. 173) gives pairs of horns and oboes and a single bassoon a chance to play the beginning of Gluck's song.

## 15

IGNACIO DE JERUSALEM (CA. 1707–1769)

# Matins for the Virgin of Guadalupe: *Vidi speciosam*
## 1764

Edited by Craig H. Russell © 1997. Reprinted with permission.

Vidi speciosam sicut columbam ascendentem
desuper rivos aquarum, cuius inestimabilis
odor erat nimis in vestimentis eius.
Et sicut dies verni circumdabant eam
flores rosarum et lilia convallium.

*I saw the fair one rising like a dove*
*above the streams of waters; her incomparable*
*fragrance was strong in her garments.*
*And as on a spring day she was surrounded by*
*flowers of roses and lily of the valley.*

Quae est ista quae ascendit per desertum
Sicut virgula fumi ex aromatibus
Myrrhae et thuris?

*Who is she that arises from the desert*
*like pillars of smoke from incense*
*of myrrh and frankincense?*

Composers of church music in Spanish America regarded the Matins service (part of the
Divine Office) as an especially attractive opportunity for composition on a grand scale. The
three large sections (nocturns) of the Matins, somewhat analogous to the three acts of an

opera, each required several pieces of orchestrally accompanied music and a wide variety of musical techniques, ranging from arias in the theatrical style to fugues. Ignacio de Jerusalem, the most important composer active in mid-eighteenth-century Mexico City, met the challenge brilliantly; clearly indicative of his compositional skill and of the musical sophistication of his Mexican congregation is the responsory *Vidi speciosam*.

Alto and bass soloists alternate with chorus, accompanied by an orchestra of strings with pairs of oboes and horns. The movement is in a dal segno form whose opening **A** section is in the expected binary form, but with an unusual excursus to the subdominant, C minor, in the first part (marked with an exclamation point below), which results in that part being more than twice as long the second part.

### *Vidi speciosam:* A section

| FORM | First Part | Second Part |
|---|---|---|
| KEY (i = G MINOR) | i–III–iv!–III | III–i |
| TEXT | Vidi speciosam | Et sicut dies verni |
| MEASURES | 1–34 | 35–50 |

After a short **B** section in E♭ major, the movement concludes with a repetition of the second part of the **A** section.

### *Vidi speciosam:* large-scale form

| FORM | A | B | A′ |
|---|---|---|---|
| KEY (i = G MINOR) | i | VI | III–i |
| TEXT | Vidi speciosam | Quae est ista | Et sicut dies verni |
| MEASURES | 1–50 | 51–57 | 35–50 |

*Vidi speciosam* shows Jerusalem to have been aware of recent stylistic developments in Europe. He cast the alto's opening tune in the modish three-measure **ABB′** form, and introduced into it an augmented-sixth chord (end of m. 6). But in the way he combined these two modern elements he departed from European convention, which generally required an **ABB′** melody to end with a V–I cadence.

Equally unconventional is the long descending sequence at measures 16–20, with melismas in all the choral parts, which nicely conveys the meaning of the Latin word *aquarum* (of waters). Its tonal destination (C minor) represents an unexpected detour in this part of the **A** section's binary structure, in which the relative major (B♭) has already been established. This choral writing, as bizarre as it is beautiful, might remind us of Haydn's claim that his isolation at Eszterháza forced him to be original. Jerusalem, separated from the centers of European music by a vast ocean and a long overland trek from Veracruz to the capital, could have made a similar claim, with greater justification.

# TOMMASO TRAETTA (1727–1779)

## *Antigona: Piangi, o Tebe*

### 1772

Edited by John A. Rice. Principal source: Western University, London, Ontario, Music Library MZ 1292.

Piangi, o Tebe, ancor t'ingombra

La funesta ombra di morte.

Non è sazia ancor la sorte

O di lacrime, o d'orror.

*Weep, Thebes: you are still beset*

*by the funereal shadow of death.*

*Fate is not yet satiated*

*with tears or with horror.*

In 1768 the prolific and adventurous composer Tommaso Traetta joined the group of distinguished Italian musicians who occupied, in turn, the position of music director at the Russian court in St. Petersburg. During the first three years of his tenure he presented mostly revisions of works he had written in Italy. But in 1772 the librettist Marco Coltellini and the soprano Caterina Gabrielli, with whom he had collaborated on some of his most innovative earlier operas, followed him to St. Petersburg. They seem to have inspired him to a new burst of creative energy, which produced one of his masterpieces: *Antigona*.

First performed in St. Petersburg on November 11, 1772, *Antigona* exemplifies Traetta's synthesis, along the lines suggested by Francesco Algarotti's *Saggio sull'opera in musica* (An Essay on the Opera, discussed in Chapter 8 of *Music in the Eighteenth Century*), of French operatic spectacle and Italian vocal virtuosity. It responded to the same aesthetic concerns embodied in Gluck's *Orfeo ed Euridice* (as illustrated in Anthology 9); but unlike *Orfeo*, *Antigona* is a full-length opera, in three acts. It offered Traetta the widest possible canvas on which to explore some of the most exciting trends in Italian opera of the third quarter of the eighteenth century.

The third and final act of *Antigona* opens with a magnificent scene-complex in which the title character, sentenced to death, bids farewell to her family and friends, and they bewail her fate. It combines chorus, dance, orchestrally accompanied recitative, and solo song within a frame supplied by the monumental chorus *Piange, o Tebe* (Weep, Thebes), which is sung twice, at the beginning and end.

*Piangi, o Tebe* reflects vividly Traetta's situation in St. Petersburg, as an Italian musician steeped in the traditions of the galant style working in the capital of a country that had its own deeply engrained musical traditions. The chorus's *form* is very much a product of the Italian galant; its *content* is a product of the choral culture that Traetta found in Russia—specifically the tradition of choral music associated with the Orthodox Church.

*Piangi, o Tebe* uses the same parallel binary form, with the text stated twice, that we have seen in so many eighteenth-century vocal works, beginning with the first movement of Giovanni Battista Pergolesi's *Stabat Mater* (see Anthology 1). In keeping with the darkness of the dramatic situation, the first part ends not in the expected relative major, G, but in its parallel minor.

| FORM | First Part | Second Part |
|---|---|---|
| KEY (i = E MINOR) | i–v–iii | III–i |
| MEASURES | 1–14 | 14–27 |

Traetta enhanced the effect of this modal substitution by repeated use of augmented-sixth harmony to underline the meaning of the words "tears" and "horror." Full of dissonance, and more contrapuntal than many eighteenth-century operatic choruses, *Piangi, o Tebe* is not easy to sing; in composing it Traetta was counting on the well-trained choristers of the Russian imperial chapel to bring it to life.

## 17

GIOVANNI PAISIELLO (1740–1816)

# *Il barbiere di Siviglia*: **Finale of Act 4 (extract)**
## 1782

From Givanni Paisiello, *Il Barbiere di Siviglia* (Milan: Ricordi).

_pa_ro, ci han le va _ ta la sca _ la di già.    Ah son i _ o la cau_sa inno_

_cen_te, tutto ho det_to, il tu_tor m'ha ingan_na_ta, e_gli sa che voi sie_te ora

qua.    Eccel _ len_za, già a _ pron la por_ta...    Ah Lin_do _ ro!    Ah Lin_

_do _ ro!    ac_cor _ re _ te,    ve _ de _ te...    Ah Ro _ si _ na! no, no, non te_

_me_te; voi mia spo_sa quest'oggi sa _ re _ te, ed il vecchio pu ni _ re sa

(Entra D. Basilio con il Notaro)    FIG.

_prò, ed il vecchio pu ni _ re sa _ prò. Ec_cel _ lenza, ecco il nostro No_

CON.    DON BASILIO

_ta _ ro. E l'a _ mi _ co Ba_si _ lio è con lu _ i. Cos'è que_sto, cos'è

NOTARO

que_sto, che co _ sa mai ve _ do? Sono que_sti gli spo_si fu_

COUNT

| | |
|---|---|
| Cara, sei tu il mio bene, | *My dear, you are my darling,* |
| L'idolo del mio cor. | *My heart's idol.* |

ROSINA

| | |
|---|---|
| Caro, fra dolci pene | *My dear, amid sweet pains,* |
| Ardo per te d'amor. | *I burn with love for you.* |

COUNT

| | |
|---|---|
| Oh Dio! Che bel contento! | *Oh God! What happiness!* |

ROSINA

| | |
|---|---|
| Che bel piacer che sento! | *What pleasure I feel!* |

BOTH

| | |
|---|---|
| Tutte le pene obblio, | *I've forgotten all our troubles,* |
| E a te, bell'idol mio, | *And to you, my love,* |
| Sarò fedele ognor. | *I will always be faithful.* |

*During the duet, Figaro looks repeatedly at the window, to avoid being taken by surprise, and at this moment he cries out:*

FIGARO

| | |
|---|---|
| Eccellenza non v'è più riparo, | *Your Excellence, there is no way out,* |
| Ci han levata la scala di già! | *They have taken away the ladder!* |

ROSINA

| | |
|---|---|
| Ah! son io la causa innocente! | *It's my fault: innocently* |
| Tutto ho detto, il tutor m'ha ingannata! | *I told everything, my guardian tricked me!* |
| Egli sa che voi siete ora qua. | *He knows we are here.* |

FIGARO

| | |
|---|---|
| Eccellenza, già apron la porta . . . | *Your Excellence, they are opening the door . . .* |

*(looking again)*

ROSINA

Ah, Lindoro! Accorrete, vedete . . .     *Lindoro! Come look . . .*

*(running into the count's arms)*

COUNT

Ah, Rosina, no, no non temete;     *Rosina, have no fear;*
Voi mia sposa quest'oggi sarete,     *You will be my wife this very day,*
Ed il vecchio punire saprò.     *And the old man will be punished.*

*(enter Basilio and a notary)*

FIGARO

Eccellenza, ecco il nostro notaro!     *Your Excellence, here is our notary!*

COUNT

E l'amico Basilio è con lui.     *And our friend Basilio is with him.*

BASILIO

Cos'è questo? Che cosa mai vedo?     *What's this? What do I see?*

NOTARY

Sono questi gli sposi futuri?     *Are these the bride and groom?*

COUNT

Siamo noi. Il contratto l'avete?     *We are. Do you have the contract?*

NOTARY

Mancan i nomi. Il contratto egli è qui.     *The names are missing. The contract is here.*

ROSINA

Io mi chiamo Rosina: scrivete!     *My name is Rosina. Write!*

*(to the notary, who writes)*

COUNT

| | |
|---|---|
| Ed il conte son io d'Almaviva. | *And I am Count Almaviva.* |
| Soscriviamo. E voi, Don Basilio, | *Let's sign. And you, Don Basilio,* |
| Testimonio sarete, lo spero. | *will be the witness, I hope.* |

*(everyone signs, except Don Basilio)*

BASILIO

| | |
|---|---|
| Ma eccellenza, . . . ma come, il dottore . . . | *But Your Excellence, the doctor . . .* |

COUNT

| | |
|---|---|
| Soscrivete, non fate il ragazzo | *Sign, and don't be a child.* |

*(tossing him a purse with gold coins)*

BASILIO

| | |
|---|---|
| Sottoscrivo | *I'll sign.* |

FIGARO

| | |
|---|---|
| (Inver non è pazzo!) | *He's not stupid!* |

BASILIO

| | |
|---|---|
| Questo è un peso che fa dir di sì. | *This weighs enough to make one say yes.* |

NOTARY, FIGARO

| | |
|---|---|
| Quello è un peso che fa dir di sì. | *That weighs enough to make one say yes.* |

COUNT, ROSINA

| | |
|---|---|
| Il danaro fa sempre così. | *Money always acts like that.* |

Giovanni Paisiello was one of the early masters of the finale, the act-ending ensemble in which most or all of an opera's characters interact with one another, and changes in the dramatic situation are communicated to the audience through changes in the music's tempo, meter, mode, and orchestration. *Il barbiere di Siviglia*, the most celebrated of the comic operas that he wrote for the court of Empress Catherine the Great, ends with a finale that takes 10 to 12 minutes to perform; this excerpt consists of roughly the first half.

The finale takes place in the bedroom of Rosina, a beautiful young woman who is being courted by Count Almaviva, but whose guardian, old Doctor Bartolo, wants to marry her himself. With the help of Figaro, Almaviva intends to elope with Rosina, and has found a way to her bedroom. The finale begins with Rosina and Almaviva declaring their love in a passage in which time seems to stand still—a gorgeously expansive duet, richly decked out with clarinets in parallel thirds. This Larghetto in B♭ and triple meter goes on for 62 measures.

Figaro interrupts the lovebirds (m. 63) to announce that the ladder placed earlier for their escape has been removed; the interruption is signaled by a new meter ($\frac{2}{4}$) and tempo (Allegro moderato). Events now move quickly to the dénouement. Bartolo, putting into effect his own plan to marry Rosina, has summoned his friend Basilio and a notary, who arrive with a marriage contract (m. 84). In a passage marked "Recitativo" (m. 98, meter: **c**), Rosina and Almaviva take advantage of Bartolo's absence to have their own names entered into the contract. Almaviva asks Basilio to serve as a witness, and Basilio's consternation at this turn of events is reflected in a shift back to $\frac{2}{4}$ meter (m. 107). Almaviva offers him money and he quickly changes his mind. The action suddenly stops (m. 120) as everyone reflects on gold's magical effect in an Andante—an adorable little march—in the subdominant, E♭: music of such delicacy and charm makes it is easy to understand how Paisiello delighted Europe. By the time of Bartolo's arrival (m. 146, Allegro, **c**, E♭; not included here), Almaviva and Rosina are safely married. A judge enters and tries to restore order (m. 182, Andante, **c**, F). Bartolo protests (m. 198, Allegro, B♭–G minor–V of B♭, but to no avail; intimidated by Almaviva's wealth and social rank, he adds his signature to the marriage contract and joins in a celebration of the happy ending (m. 268, Allegro, **c**, B♭).

## 18

WOLFGANG AMADEUS MOZART (1756–1791)

# Piano Concerto No. 17 in G Major, K. 453: Movement 2
## 1784

From Wolfgang Amadeus Mozart, *Piano Concertos Nos. 17–22 in Full Score* (New York: Dover Publications, Inc.).

Although Wolfgang Amadeus Mozart wrote most of his 17 Viennese piano concertos with the intention of performing them himself in concert, he wrote a few of them for some of Vienna's best female pianists. For his talented student Barbara Ployer he composed the Concerto No. 17 in G Major, K. 453. He finished it in April 1784 and two months later she played it at a private concert at her parents' house in Döbling, in the suburbs of Vienna. The concert also included a performance of Mozart's Quintet for Piano and Winds, K. 452, in which he played the piano part, and the Sonata for Two Pianos, K. 448, which he and Ployer played together.

The relaxed, pastoral atmosphere of the concerto's first and third movements made it particularly appropriate for performance in verdant Döbling, where birdsong in the surrounding fields and woods might have complemented the birdlike trills of the woodwinds. But the slow movement presents darker, more intimate and enigmatic images.

In this sublime C-major Andante, Mozart used sonata form to explore a wide range of instrumental sonorities, melodic styles, and harmonic areas. Indeed, the conventional solidity of the movement's large-scale binary structure and tonal plan gave Mozart the freedom to innovate in other musical directions.

| BINARY FORM | First Part | | Second Part | |
| --- | --- | --- | --- | --- |
| SONATA FORM | Orchestral introduction | Exposition | Development | Recapitulation |
| KEY (I = C) | I | I–V | V ◊◊◊◊ | I |
| MEASURES | 1–29 | 30–64 | 64–90 | 90–135 |

The Andante begins with an orchestral introduction that presents some elements that will have important roles in the movement as a whole. The first theme (mm. 1–5) combines the rhythmic and metrical conventions of the sarabande with the voice-leading conventions of the romanesca. By alluding to the first movement's second theme, this tune encourages listeners to hear the Andante as emerging from—and a kind of extension of—the first movement. But here the melody (unlike its cousin in the first movement) is oddly short, seemingly truncated. With the opening theme left incomplete, the winds take over, introducing themselves as a second crucial ingredient of the Andante; yet a third is the minor mode, introduced in the closing material at measures 25–29.

The exposition proper begins with the entrance of the piano at measure 30. Here again the first theme is left unfinished. In the modulatory passage that begins at measure 35, the pianist takes the lead by plunging into G minor, thus beginning to fulfill the promise that the passage at measures 25–29 made about the importance of the minor mode in the movement to follow. Together with the incompleteness of the opening melody, this emphasis on the minor contributes to a prevailing sense of instability and unease. The second melodic area (mm. 42–54) offers a respite. It begins with a ravishing dialogue of wind instruments. The piano takes up the wind's ascending arpeggio and extends it into a lovely Prinner that unfolds slowly, over four measures (mm. 47–50). Mozart delayed every note in the $\hat{6}$–$\hat{5}$–$\hat{4}$–$\hat{3}$ melodic descent except the last by means of appoggiaturas, wringing every possible drop of expressive potential from the old voice-leading schema.

The return of the truncated first theme, played by the winds in G major (mm. 64–68), announces the beginning of the development—a passage of remarkable harmonic adventurousness. In the piano's tragic solo in D minor, the repeated eighth-note Ds have an effect similar to that of the softly pulsating As at the beginning of the slow movement of Saint-Georges's Violin Concerto in D Major (see Anthology 6). D minor gives way to an area of tonal instability that ultimately reaches the exceedingly remote tonal realm of C♯ minor. Then, in this movement's most dramatic moment, a modulation whose apparent miraculousness is emphasized by a crescendo brings us suddenly back to the tonic; the recapitulation begins at measure 90 with a double return.

But the harmonic surprises are not over yet; having reestablished C major, the music delves suddenly, at the beginning of the connecting passage, into E♭ major, ratcheting up one more turn the sense of disorientation that this movement conveys. By another harmonic slight of hand, Mozart redefines A♭, the fourth scale degree in E♭ major, as the lowest note in an augmented-sixth chord that resolves to the dominant of C, thus preparing for the second melodic area, now in C major. The unexpectedly late excursion away from the tonic finds compensation near the end of the movement (mm. 123–30), when the opening melody—in C major, of course—is finally presented in its complete form. Thus the movement's melodic puzzle is finally solved, just as its extraordinary harmonic adventure comes to an end.

## 19

JOSEPH HAYDN (1732–1809)

# String Quartet in E♭ Major, Op. 33, No. 2 ("The Joke"): Movement 4

## 1781

From Joseph Haydn, Quartet No. 38 in E♭ Major, Op. 33, No. 2 (London: Ernst Eulenberg).

In 1779, as Joseph Haydn approached the twentieth anniversary of his engagement by the Esterházy princes, he signed a contract extension that made an important change to the conditions that he had agreed to two decades earlier: a change that tacitly acknowledged the fame he had won throughout Europe. Although his earlier contract (quoted in *Music in the Eighteenth Century*, Chapter 10) prohibited him from composing "for any other person without the knowledge and gracious permission" of Prince Esterházy, Haydn had in fact composed several sets of string quartets during the early 1770s with publication in mind. But the deletion of that restriction in 1779 allowed him to strengthen his relations with publishers and to increase the amount of time and energy he devoted to the composition of music for publication.

One of the first fruits of the expansion of artistic independence that Haydn enjoyed from 1779 was the set of six string quartets that the Viennese publisher Artaria issued in 1782 as Opus 33. Haydn described these quartets as having been "composed in an entirely new and special way."

The String Quartet in Eb Major, later nicknamed "The Joke," ends with a movement to which he assigned the tempo Presto. This finale begins by leading listeners to expect that the form of the movement will be that of a rondo, in which a theme in the tonic is stated several times in alternation with contrasting material that explores other keys. Eighteenth-century composers frequently used the rondo as the final movement of an instrumental work; an earlier example is the third movement of Saint-Georges's Violin Concerto in D Major (see Anthology 6). This being the last movement in the quartet, listeners probably expected it to be a rondo, and their expectation was strengthened by the character and form of the opening theme.

Binary form served eighteenth-century composers as a structure not only for whole movements but also for melodies. This movement's main theme is in rounded binary form, with both parts repeated. Haydn greatly extended the length of the second half of the binary structure by delaying the return of the opening idea (a return that he led listeners to start waiting for by means of a dominant pedal at m. 16). This is the first of several ways in which Haydn, in keeping with a tendency evident throughout the quartets of Opus 33, disconcerted and amused players and listeners alike by establishing expectations and then manipulating them: promising something and delaying its arrival (or delivering something else).

Having established the tonic, eighteenth-century composers modulated almost automatically to the dominant. Haydn undermined expectations again by moving instead to the subdominant (Ab) and a melody accompanied by a drone that makes it sound like a peasant dance.

After the second statement of the main theme (without repeats), we expect a shift to a darker musical color at the beginning of the second episode, in which eighteenth-century composers often used the minor mode. But Haydn had yet another surprise in store, staying in the tonic and laying down a tonic pedal that makes this music sound like the beginning of a coda (m. 108). This might cause us to rethink what we have heard so far: not the beginning of a rondo but a movement in ternary form (**ABA'**–coda).

The uncertainty and disorientation that we might feel is momentarily allayed when a dominant pedal (approached by means of the converging cadence at mm. 127–28) leads us to expect a third statement of the main theme. This expectation is, for once, satisfied (mm. 141–48); the appearance of this theme removes any lingering doubts about the movement being a rondo, but introduces a new puzzle: only the first part of the melody is played before a sudden change of tempo, from Presto to Adagio, presents a cadence in which the first violin, repeating the end of the melody, transforms it into a tender farewell. With this surprising, amusing, but touching close, the movement seems to have come to an end (at m. 152).

But by now we should be aware of trusting our expectations. And indeed the movement is not over. After a moment of silence, the main theme begins again in the fast tempo—or tries to begin. Each phrase is separated by rests, so that what had originally been an 8-measure period now takes 14 measures to finish. With this cadence (m. 166) we come to what is surely the quartet's much delayed conclusion. Or is it?

| FORM | A | B | A′ | C | A′ |
|---|---|---|---|---|---|
| KEY (I = E♭) | I | IV! | I | I! | I |
| MEASURES | 1–36 | 37–71 | 72–107 | 108–140 | 141–? |

# String Quartet in A Major, K. 464: Movement 2

## 1785

From Wolfgang Amadeus Mozart, *Complete String Quartets* (New York: Dover Publications, Inc.).

M.D.C.

Mozart wrote no string quartets between 1774 and 1781: a major gap when one considers the brevity of his career and the number of major works in other genres that he wrote during the second half of the 1770s. His return to the string quartet during his early years in Vienna was a response, above all, to the publication in 1782 of Joseph Haydn's Opus 33 quartets (see Anthology 19). The popularity of Haydn's set brought new prestige to the genre, and its musical sophistication must have fascinated and stimulated the younger composer. But unlike Haydn, who composed the six quartets of Opus 33 in a single creative burst during the second half of 1781, Mozart accumulated his quartets slowly, over the course of two years. Particularly busy as a performer in concerts, he had to give compositional priority to works he could himself perform in public, especially piano concertos. This meant that his response to Haydn's Opus 33 took the form of a long-term project. He began with the Quartet in G Major, K. 387, finished in December 1782, and completed the set of six with the Quartet in C Major, K. 465, in January 1785. Artaria, the Viennese music publisher who had issued Haydn's set, published Mozart's quartets in a handsome edition dedicated to Haydn. In his dedication, Mozart famously referred to his quartets as "the fruit of long and laborious effort." They have come to be known, a little confusingly, as Mozart's "Haydn" Quartets.

Like the quartets by Haydn that inspired them, the quartets that Mozart dedicated to Haydn are all in four movements. Although four-movement symphonies usually place the minuet third, between the slow movement and the finale, the string quartet gave composers the option of putting the minuet before the slow movement. Thus Mozart, in the "Haydn" Quartets, placed the minuet in the second position in three quartets and in the third position in three others. In the String Quartet in A Major, K. 464, which Mozart completed in January 1785, the minuet is the second movement. It exemplifies the ingenuity with which Mozart combined the galant and learned styles in these quartets.

The minuet was a strange phenomenon in eighteenth-century music: the only one of the French ballroom dances of the previous century to maintain a crucial role in instrumental music, it preserved through the eighteenth century and into the nineteenth the seventeenth-century practice of presenting two dances of the same type in **ABA** form, with the second dance coming to be known as the trio. Because both the minuet and the trio are (as dance movements) in binary form, their assembly into a larger ternary structure is analogous to the use of a binary **A** section within the da capo and dal segno arias, as exemplified by Giovanni Battista Pergolesi's *A Serpina penserete* and Johann Adolf Hasse's *Per questo dolce amplesso* (see Anthology 2 and 3). Mozart's A-major minuet and its trio in E major are both in rounded binary form.

| FORM | A | | B | | A | |
|---|---|---|---|---|---|---|
| | Minuet | | Trio | | Minuet | |
| | ‖: a :‖ | ‖: ba′ :‖ | ‖: c :‖ | ‖: dc′ :‖ | ‖: a :‖ | ‖: ba′ :‖ |
| KEY (I = A) | I–V | V–I | V | II–V | I–V | V–I |
| MEASURES | 1–28 | 29–72 | 73–80 | 81–104 | 1–28 | 29–72 |

The minuet begins with two completely different melodic ideas in quick succession, each consisting of a two-measure phrase repeated in sequence: idea 1 in octaves (mm. 1–4), and idea 2—an elaboration of the $\hat{5}$–$\hat{4}$–$\hat{3}$ descent from which Mozart derived thematic material for every movement of this quartet—in the first violin with accompaniment in the second violin and viola (mm. 5–8). Mozart subjected this simple material to increasingly intricate contrapuntal treatment. First, ideas 1 and 2 are played simultaneously (mm. 9–12), then idea 1 in canonic imitation (mm. 13–17), then idea 2 in canon (mm. 17–21), and finally—the contrapuntal climax—idea 2 in canon while idea 1 is played simultaneously (mm. 59–62). No wonder the great twentieth-century composer Arnold Schoenberg, whose scores are notable for their contrapuntal intricacy, wrote admiringly of this minuet in his *Fundamentals of Musical Composition*.

The trio, in E major, presents a galant respite from the intensive contrapuntal display. The descending cello line alludes to the romanesca that we have seen in Domenico Gallo's Trio Sonata No. 1 in G Major (see Anthology 7) and the slow movement of Mozart's Piano Concerto in G Major (see Anthology 18). The first violin carries the tune, with the second violin occasionally in parallel thirds. That tune includes the $\hat{5}$–$\hat{4}$–$\hat{3}$ melodic descent (mm. 76–77) here in a chromatic version that anticipates the beginning of the finale.

# Così fan tutte: Fra gli amplessi in pochi istanti

## 1790

From Wolfgang Amadeus Mozart, *Cosi fan tutte* (New York: C.F. Peters).

| FIORDILIGI | Fra gli amplessi in pochi istanti | *In a few moments I will reach* |
| | Giungerò del fido sposo; | *the embrace of my faithful lover;* |
| | Sconosciuta a lui davanti | *unrecognized in this outfit* |
| | In quest' abito verrò. | *I will come to him.* |
| | Oh che gioa il suo bel core | *Oh what joy his heart* |
| | Proverà nel ravvirsarmi! | *will feel when he sees me!* |

| FERRANDO | Ed intanto di dolore | *And in the meantime* |
| | Meschinello io mi morrò. | *I will die of sorrow* |

| FIORDILIGI | Cosa veggio? Son tradita! | *What do I see? I'm betrayed!* |
| | Deh partite . . . | *Please leave!* |

| FERRANDO | Ah no, mia vita. | *No, my darling.* |
| | Con quel ferro di tua mano | *With this sword, and by your hand,* |
| | Questo cor tu ferirai, | *you will pierce my heart,* |
| | E se forza oh Dio non hai, | *and if you do not have the strength,* |
| | Io la man ti reggerò. | *I will guide your hand.* |

*(he takes the sword from the table and unsheathes it)*

| FIORDILIGI | Taci ahimè, son abbastanza | *Be silent. I am* |
| | Tormentata ed infelice! | *tortured and unhappy enough.* |

| FIORDILIGI⎫ | Ah che omai la mia (sua) costanza | *Already my (her) resistence,* |
| FERRANDO ⎭ | A quei sguardi, a quel che dice, | *in the face of his (my) looks and words,* |
| | Incomincia a vacillar. | *is beginning to weaken.* |

| FIORDILIGI | Sorgi, sorgi. . . | *Get up, get up . . .* |
| FERRANDO | Invan lo credi. | *You ask in vain.* |
| FIORDILIGI | Per pietà, da me che chiedi? | *What do you want from me?* |
| FERRANDO | Il tuo cor, o la mia morte. | *Your heart, or my death.* |
| FIORDILIGI | Ah non son, non son più forte. | *Ah, I am losing my strength.* |
| FERRANDO | Cedi cara. . . | *Yield, my love. . .* |

*(he takes her hand, and kisses it)*

| FIORDILIGI | Dei consiglio! | *Gods, give me advice!* |
| FERRANDO | Volgi a me pietoso il ciglio, | *Give me a look of pity;* |
| | In me sol trovar tu puoi | *in me alone you will find* |
| | Sposo, amante, e più se vuoi, | *husband, lover, and more, if you want;* |
| | Idol mio, più non tardar. | *my darling, do not delay any longer.* |

*(with the utmost tenderness)*

| FIORDILIGI | Giusto ciel! Crudel, hai vinto, | *Good God! Cruel man, you have won.* |
| | Fa di me quel che ti par. | *Do whatever you want with me.* |
| FIORDILIGI ⎫ | Abbracciamci, o caro bene, | *Let us embrace, my love,* |
| FERRANDO ⎭ | E un conforto a tante pene | *and let us put an end to so much pain* |
| | Sia languir di dolce affetto, | *by languishing in sweet feelings* |
| | Di diletto sospirar. | *and sighing with pleasure.* |

(*exeunt*)

In the second act of *Così fan tutte* (All Women Act Like That), Ferrando and Guglielmo, Italian military officers who have disguised themselves as Albanians, try to seduce each other's financées, confident that the women will repel their advances (and that they will thereby win their bet with Don Alfonso). Guglielmo's Fiordiligi remains faithful at first, but Ferrando's Dorabella gives in to Guglielmo surprisingly quickly. Ferrando, jealous and humiliated (and no longer caring about the bet), intensifies his pursuit of Fiordiligi, which reaches its climax in the duet *Fra gli amplessi in pochi istanti*.

Mozart's librettist Lorenzo Da Ponte laid out the duet in a poem of 34 lines, whose structure, like that of the text of *Madamina, il catalogo è questo* (see Anthology 23), gave Mozart the basis for his musical structure. The duet falls into four sections, each with a different tempo:

| TEMPO | Adagio | Allegro | Larghetto | Andante |
|---|---|---|---|---|
| KEY (I = A) | I–V/III | III–V/i | I | I |
| TEXT (LINES) | 1–9 | 9–24 | 25–30 | 31–34 |
| MEASURES | 1–23 | 24–75 | 76–101 | 101–142 |

The first three sections depict, step by step, Ferrando's seduction of Fiordiligi, and the fourth depicts the lovers' anticipation of erotic bliss.

The duet, preceded by a recitative in which Fiordiligi resolves to dress up as a soldier and seek Guglielmo on the battlefield, begins as if it were an aria for the soprano. Both text and music, in A major, are completely serious. Earlier in the opera Alfonso undermined the seriousness of some of Mozart's ensembles; here Ferrando interrupts, telling Fiordiligi that he will die in misery if she rejects his advances. Ferrando's sudden entrance is accompanied by a shift from major to minor. The projection of a change in the dramatic situation by a tonal shift is a technique typical of opera buffa.

Fiordiligi reacts to Ferrando's appearance with shock, conveyed by Mozart with a change of tempo (from Adagio to Allegro) and a more active accompaniment, and yet another key change: to the more distant realm of C major. (The importance of the relationship of C major to A major in this duet anticipates the crucial role that third-relations—relations between keys that are a minor or major third apart, such as C major and E major, or C major and A♭ major—would play in nineteenth-century music.)

Ferrando, as if refusing to let Fiordiligi escape, follows her into C major. His melody is full of irony for the audience: he sang much the same music near the beginning of the opera, in the same key, to the words "I want to organize a beautiful serenade for my goddess" (see Ex. 14.8 in *Music in the Eighteenth Century*). Now he serenades another goddess, probably with more intensity than he ever summoned for Dorabella. Fiordiligi steers the tonality toward the dominant of A, seemingly encouraging Ferrando with a question to which she already knows the answer: "What do you want from me?" She gives the dominant of A one final reiteration, asking the gods for advice. But it is of course Ferrando, sensing now that she is ready to be convinced, who answers her plea, in the gorgeous A-major Larghetto *Volgi a me pietoso il ciglio* (Give me a look of pity).

The Larghetto, a musical caress of unsurpassed sweetness and warmth, sounds so sincere in its promise of happiness and pleasure that it puts Fiordiligi over the edge. Ferrando never has a chance to finish tonally; it is Fiordiligi who has the last word (and the perfect cadence): "Do whatever you want with me." Mozart depicted the actual moment of Fiordiligi's capitulation, at the very end of the Larghetto, with a lyrical oboe melody and a cadence as inevitable as it is beautiful.

In the duet's concluding Andante, solidly in tonic A major, Fiordiligi and Ferrando sing in parallel thirds and sixths and later intertwine in imitation, apparently unanimous in their happiness. But we need to keep in mind that they are happy about completely different things. Ferrando, in expressing love for Fiordiligi, continues to deceive her; in reality he rejoices that he has paid back Guglielmo for seducing Dorabella (and paid back Dorabella for giving in to Guglielmo); only Fiordiligi celebrates her new relationship and joyfully anticipates its sexual consummation. That consummation will presumably never happen: Ferrando will soon remove his disguise, revealing to Fiordiligi that his seduction was all play-acting.

# Symphony No. 38 in D Major, K. 504 (*Prague*): Movement 1
## 1786

From Wolfgang Amadeus Mozart. *Later Symphonies (Nos.35–41) in Full Score* (New York: Dover Publications, Inc.).

Mozart finished the grand Symphony in D Major, K. 504, in December 1786, entering its opening bars in his catalogue of works under the date December 6. It has become known as the *Prague* Symphony because of the strong possibility that it was one of the symphonies performed in the concert that he gave in Prague the following month. The symphony consists of three movements, all of them in sonata form.

With a massive and solemn slow introduction that emphasizes the minor mode, Mozart announced the monumental scope and content of this symphony. Yet once the Allegro begins, the exposition's first melodic area gives the impression of hesitancy, almost as if Mozart were casting about for ideas. This music offers us a glimpse of the act of musical invention: it seems to take shape as we hear it. The apparently aimless syncopations only gradually coalesce into something like a theme (characterized by repeated eighth notes) in measure 41. The sense of improvisation—of something spontaneously taking shape—is enhanced by Mozart's use of a Prinner (mm. 41–43) in which the $\hat{6}$–$\hat{5}$–$\hat{4}$–$\hat{3}$ melodic descent is broken up between the second violins (which play $\hat{6}$–$\hat{5}$) and the first violins (which play $\hat{4}$–$\hat{3}$).

## Overall structure

| FORM | | | First Part | Second Part | |
|---|---|---|---|---|---|
| | | Slow introduction | ‖ Exposition ‖ | Development | Recapitulation |
| KEY | | I–V/I | I–V | V ⋀⋁⋀ V/I | I |
| MEASURES | | 1–36 | 37–142 | 143–207 | 208–302 |

## Exposition

| FORM | Melodic area 1 | Modulatory passage | Melodic area 2 | Closing material |
|---|---|---|---|---|
| KEY (I = D) | I | I–V/V | V–v–V | V |
| MEASURES | 37–51 | 51–96 | 97–121 | 121–42 |

The first connecting passage in the exposition begins at measure 51, with a new idea in the first violins serving as a counterpoint to the repeated eighth-note motive from the first melodic area.

Does the second melodic area begin at measure 71 or at measure 97? The suddenly reduced orchestration at measure 70, the change in dynamics from *forte* to *piano*, and the reappearance (now in the dominant) of material from the first melodic area can all be cited to support an argument that the second melodic area begins here. On the other hand, as the passage continues it takes on the character of connecting or modulatory material, suggesting that it might be better to think of the passage beginning at measure 70 as a melodic interpolation within a larger modulatory area that extends all the way through measure 96.

The melody that begins at measure 97 has a much more balanced phrase structure than anything heard so far in this movement: eight measures plus eight measures. The sudden shift from major to minor at the tune's halfway point is anticipated by the shift from major to minor in the slow introduction. Mozart's characteristic melodic prolixity encouraged him to add a second melody in the dominant, which the violins begin as a counterpoint to the bassoons' presentation of part of the first melody (mm. 112–15) and then continue as a completely new and independent theme (but still part of the second melodic area). The cadential material that follows (from m. 121) is based largely on ideas from the first melodic area (including the syncopations from the beginning) and the modulatory area.

The development subjects to polyphonic treatment a motive (two half notes an octave apart, the second tied to the first of a descending scale of eighth notes) from the wind fanfare in the first melodic area. (Mozart was to explore the contrapuntal implications of a very similar motive in the first movement of his last symphony, the *Jupiter* of 1788.) Later in the development Mozart combined this idea with other material from the first melodic area in a dazzling display of counterpoint. A false recapitulation at measure 189 (the opening theme, but not in the tonic) leads by way of an augmented-sixth chord (m. 194) to a dominant pedal that underpins a beautifully crafted transition back to D major.

The recapitulation proper, beginning at measure 208, avoids any hint of the perfunctory. Mozart entirely recomposed the connecting passage, removing from it the structural ambiguity of the analogous music in the exposition; there is no longer any question about where the second melodic area begins (at m. 244). He also expanded the closing material (beginning at m. 270), intensifying its dramatic effect by the addition of chromatic harmony and exploitation of the violins' high register.

## 23

# WOLFGANG AMADEUS MOZART (1756–1791)

## *Don Giovanni: Madamina, il catalogo è questo*
### 1787

From Wolfgang Amadeus Mozart, *Don Giovanni Vocal Score* (New York: Dover Publications).

non si pic - ca, se sia ric - ca, se sia brut - ta, se sia

bel - la, se sia ric - ca, brut-ta, se sia bel - la, pur - chè __

por - ti la __ gon-nel - la; voi sa - pe - te

quel che fa, voi sa - pe - te quel che

| | |
|---|---|
| Madamina, il catalogo è questo | *Young lady, this is the catalogue* |
|  Delle belle che amò il padron mio, | * of the women my master has loved,* |
|  Un catalogo egli è che ho fatto io; | * a catalogue I made myself:* |
|  Osservate, leggete con me. | * look and read with me.* |
| In Italia seicento e quaranta, | *In Italy, six hundred and forty,* |
|  In Almagna duecento e trent'una, | * in Germany, two hundred and thirty-one,* |
|  Cento in Francia, in Turchia novant'una, | * one hundred in France, in Turkey ninety-one,* |
|  Ma in Ispagna son già mille e tre. | * but in Spain, one thousand and three.* |
| V'han fra queste contadine, | *Among these are peasants,* |
|  Cameriere, cittadine, | * servants, citizens,* |
|  V'han contesse, baronesse, | * countesses, baronesses,* |
|  Marchesane, principesse, | * marchionesses, princesses:* |
|  E v'han donne d'ogni grado, | * there are women of every class,* |
|  D'ogni forma, d'ogni età. | * every shape, and every age.* |
| Nella bionda egli ha l'usanza | *With the blond, he uses the technique* |
|  Di lodarla la gentilezza, | * of praising her kindness;* |
|  Nella bruna, la costanza, | * with the brunette, her constancy;* |
|  Nella bianca la dolcezza; | * with the light-skinned, her sweetness.* |
|  Vuol d'inverno la grassotta, | * In the winter he likes plumpness,* |
|  Vuol d'estate la magrotta, | * in the summer thinness,* |
|  E la grande maestosa, | * the tall, majestic woman,* |
|  La piccina è ognor vezzosa; | * and the little one is always pleasant.* |
|  Delle vecchie fa conquista | * He makes conquests of old women* |
|  Pel piacer di porle in lista, | * just for the pleasure of putting them in the list.* |
|  Sua passion predominante | * But his favorite target of all* |
|  È la giovin principiante; | * is the young beginner.* |
|  Non si picca se sia ricca, | * It matters not if she is rich,* |
|  Se sia brutta, se sia bella; | * if she is ugly or beautiful:* |
|  Purchè porti la gonnella | * as long as she wears a skirt,* |
|  Voi sapete quel che fa. | * you know what he will do.* |

In Act 1 of *Don Giovanni*, Donna Elvira confronts the man who once seduced her and whom she still loves. To escape her, Don Giovanni leaves her in the hands of his servant Leporello, who tries to console her by telling her what his master is really like. He shows her a book with the names of all Giovanni's conquests and summarizes its contents in a brilliant comic aria. Comic, yes: but it is hard to hear this aria without thinking of all the lies that Giovanni has told in seducing these women, and all the disappointment and heartache that the women have felt after being abandoned by him.

The catalogue aria—that is, an aria containing a list of people, places, or things—was a standard element in eighteenth-century Italian comic opera, almost always sung by a *buffo* (a man who specialized in comic roles). In Giovanni Paisiello's *Il barbiere di Siviglia* (The

Barber of Seville, first performed in St. Petersburg in 1782 and soon after that—to great acclaim—in Vienna), Figaro sings a brilliant aria, *Scorsi già molti paesi* (I have passed through many lands), in which he lists all the parts of Spain that he has visited. With *Madamina, il catalogo è questo*, Mozart built on and surpassed Paisiello's achievement.

For catalogue arias, librettists traditionally supplied unusually long texts, allowing the composer (and singer) to go through the text quickly and with relatively little repetition. Mozart's librettist Lorenzo Da Ponte supplied him with a text of 30 lines, the first eight consisting of 10 syllables each, and the rest consisting of 8 syllables each. He further divided the poem into four stanzas, signaling the end of each stanza with an accented syllable:

Stanza 1: lines 1–4 (10 syllables)

Stanza 2: lines 5–8 (10 syllables)

Stanza 3: lines 9–14 (8 syllables)

Stanza 4: lines 15–30 (8 syllables)

This poetic organization served Mozart as the basis for the large-scale structure of the aria.

Many eighteenth-century arias, especially in opera buffa, start with a slow section and conclude with a fast one. Paisiello, in *Scorsi già*, took the much more unusual course of beginning with a fast section in duple meter and then shifting to slow music in triple meter. Mozart did the same. His opening Allegro modulates to the dominant and ends there, as if this were the first part of a binary-form movement. The Andante con moto stays in the tonic.

| FORM | First Part | Second Part |
|---|---|---|
| TEMPO | Allegro | Andante con moto |
| KEY (I – D) | I–V | I |
| TEXT (LINES) | 1–14 | 15–30 |
| MEASURES | 1–84 | 85–172 |

The main expressive point of the Allegro is to emphasize the sheer quantity of women seduced by Giovanni. The fast tempo and the repeated eighth-note chords that dominate the accompaniment help to convey this idea, as does the patter (very fast declamation of text with many short notes, often on one pitch) with which Leporello describes the contents of his list.

In the second part of the aria (Andante con moto), Leporello emphasizes the diversity of Giovanni's women, and part of the reason for the slower tempo is simply to allow the singer and the audience to savor this diversity. It begins in—and occasionally returns to—the style of a gentle minuet, which suggests the suavity with which Giovanni exerted his charms. This passage is galant in two senses of the word: it projects masculine charm and seductiveness ("gallantry") with music whose balanced two-measure phrases, homophonic texture, parallel thirds, and slow harmonic rhythm epitomize the galant style.

Into this minuet-like framework Mozart introduced a variety of musical details that depict the size, shape, and age of the women whom Giovanni has seduced. For example, he dramatized the idea of the tall, majestic woman by accompanying the words "e la grande maestosa" with a massive crescendo of the whole orchestra, a gradually ascending line, and at the climax a pompous, fanfare-like alternation of tonic and dominant chords (mm. 106–115). The tonal stability of this part of the aria (in the tonic throughout) enhances the effect of the only departure from D major. A momentary shift to D minor—the key, already foreshadowed in the overture, that will accompany Giovanni's destruction at the end of the opera—casts a menacing shadow over Leporello's reference to Giovanni's fondness for young virgins (mm. 131–135).

◎ Norton Opera Sampler video available

## 24

JOSEPH HAYDN (1732–1809)

# Symphony No. 97 in C Major: Movement 2

## 1792

From Joseph Haydn, *London Symphonies Nos. 93–98 in Full Score* (New York: Dover Publications, Inc.).

Archi

Ob.

Haydn wrote his Symphony No. 97 for his second season of concerts in London, from February to May 1792. In the four-movement format to which he had remained faithful since the early 1760s, the symphony comprises a sonata-form movement (Vivace) preceded by a slow introduction, a slow movement (Adagio ma non troppo), a minuet (Allegretto), and a finale (Presto assai). Haydn scored the symphony for pairs of flutes, oboes, bassoons, horns, trumpets, timpani, and strings. (Although clarinets were available in London, Haydn did not find a place for them in his symphonic ensemble until his return visit in 1794–95.)

In writing the slow movement of a symphony, especially a symphony as heavily orchestrated as this one, Haydn and his contemporaries generally called for fewer winds and brass than in the faster movements that surround it, and left the timpanist with nothing to do for a few minutes. Haydn manipulated this convention in several of the symphonies he wrote for London. In Symphony No. 97 he gave the trumpets and drums, which have such an important role in the first, third, and fourth movements, an equally crucial role in the Adagio, but he kept them silent until about halfway through the movement. Thus he lulled the audience into expecting the lighter orchestration that it associated with slow movements and enhanced the effect of the trumpets and drums when they eventually sound.

This slow movement consists of a theme, three variations, and a coda. The theme is in binary form, but neither the parallel nor the rounded binary forms that were so common in the eighteenth century. The two parts of the melody are different, but they have the same character and much the same rhythmic material. As with many binary-form instrumental melodies, both parts are repeated; but instead of using repeat signs Haydn wrote out the repeats and used them as an opportunity for further variation—that is, variation *within* the theme: **aa′bb′**. The combination of duple meter and dotted rhythms gives the theme something of the effect of a slow march. It ends with an appoggiatura—C resolving down a fifth to tonic F—whose eccentricity makes it memorable. That memorability is important, because appoggiaturas play an important role later in the movement.

| FORM | Theme | Variation 1 | Variation 2 | Variation 3 | Coda |
|---|---|---|---|---|---|
| MELODIC STRUCTURE | **a a′ b b′** | **a b** | ‖a ‖ ‖b a ‖ | **a a′ b b′** | |
| PREDOMINANT RHYTHM | dotted | triplets | dotted | sixteenths | slurred pairs of eighths |
| MODE | major | major | minor | major | major |
| MEASURES | 1–44 | 45–66 | 67–84 | 85–128 | 128–149 |

Each of the three variations that follow treats the theme's structure differently. Variation 1, a study in triplets, ignores the repeats. Variation 2, in F minor, uses repeat signs and recasts the melody in rounded binary form. Only variation 3 returns to the "variation-within-the-theme" strategy exemplified by the theme itself.

Variation 3, with an almost constant flow of sixteenth notes in the strings, mirrors variation 1, with its constant triplets. This symmetry makes variation 2 the center of the movement. The sudden entry of the trumpets and timpani, the shift to the parallel minor, and violent changes in dynamics work together to make variation 2 the movement's emotional core.

A deceptive cadence at the end of variation 3 leads to an expansive coda that, growing out of the appoggiatura at the end of the theme, consists largely of an exploration of appoggiaturas and their various harmonic contexts. Some resolve down, some up; the note on the strong beat increases in length from an eighth note to a quarter note, and finally to a double appoggiatura in the winds, involving two whole notes tied together (E and G eventually resolving up to F and A as part of a tonic chord), while other, shorter appoggiaturas in the strings resolve simultaneously.

## 25

JOSEPH HAYDN (1732–1809)

# Piano Sonata No. 52 in E♭ Major, Hob. XVI-52: Movement 1
## 1794

From Joseph Haydn, *Complete Piano Sonatas,* vol. 2 (New York: Dover Publications, Inc.).

The renewed interest in the piano that Haydn showed during his second visit to London (1794–95) resulted in several piano trios (for piano, violin, and cello) and in his final three piano sonatas. He wrote at least two of these sonatas for Therese Jansen, a member of the London Pianoforte School, the group of pianists and pianist-composers who made London Europe's most productive center of keyboard composition and performance in the 1790s.

The opening Allegro of the Piano Sonata in E♭ Major is one of Haydn's grandest sonata-form movements.

| FORM | First Part | Second Part | |
| --- | --- | --- | --- |
| | Exposition | Development | Recapitulation |
| KEY (I = E♭) | I–V | ᜕᜕᜕ | I |
| MEASURES | 1–43 | 44–78 | 79–116 |

The movement begins with a voice-leading schema—a line with the scale degrees $\hat{1}$–$\flat\hat{7}$–$\hat{6}$–$\natural\hat{7}$–$\hat{1}$ over a tonic pedal—that plays an important role in the movement and (when it returns at the end of the second movement) contributes to the coherence of the sonata as a whole. In its first statement (mm. 1–2), the characteristic V-shaped line is an inner part, but it soon reveals itself more openly (mm. 6–7) in the context of rhythmic and accompanimental patterns that will be subject to much developmental manipulation later in the movement.

A repetition of the opening idea in measure 9 serves to launch the modulatory passage, which quickly reaches a dominant pedal (V of V), frequently used by Haydn and his contemporaries to signal an approach to the second melodic area (m. 14). A statement of the first theme's opening motive in B♭ (m. 17) can indeed be heard as the beginning of the second melodic area (and an example of Haydn's characteristic melodic economy), but the passage-work in the next several measures sounds more like connecting material, and seems to be on the verge of modulating away from B♭. We feel a much stronger sense of tonal stability with the statement of a quirky new theme in B♭ at measure 27, with open fifths in the accompaniment that must have reminded Haydn's listeners of a pair of horns. That theme tempts us, in retrospect, to hear everything from measure 9 to the downbeat of measure 27 as a modulatory passage. (We encountered a similar structural ambiguity in the first movement of Mozart's *Prague* Symphony; see Anthology 22.)

The big chords with which the movement begins are never heard in the long development, yet the $\hat{1}$–♭$\hat{7}$–$\hat{6}$–♮$\hat{7}$–$\hat{1}$ line is very much present. For example, the development begins with chords in which the $\hat{1}$–♭$\hat{7}$–$\hat{6}$ melodic descent is transferred to the bass, and harmonized so that A♭, the flat seventh degree in the key of B♭, serves as part of an augmented-sixth chord that resolves to a G-major chord, the dominant of C. This sets up a statement of the second theme in C major; its quirkiness is now compounded by its sounding in this unexpected key. Further modulatory adventures lead eventually to another statement of this theme, but in the even more remote key of E major (m. 68). Like Mozart's duet *Fra gli amplessi in pochi istanti* (see Anthology 21), this movement testifies to the eagerness of late-eighteenth-century composers to exploit tonal relationships beyond those (such as tonic to dominant and minor to relative major) that had yielded so many musical beauties during the previous decades.

## 26

LUDWIG VAN BEETHOVEN (1770–1827)

# Piano Sonata in A Major, Op. 2, No. 2: Movement 4
## 1796

From *Ludwig van Beethovens Werke*, Series XVI, Volume 1 (Leipzig: Breitkopf und Härtel).

One of Beethoven's first major musical publications was the set of three piano sonatas, dedicated to Haydn, that appeared in 1796. Although he departed from the normal practice of Haydn and Mozart by composing these sonatas in four movements instead of three, he followed late-eighteenth-century taste in favoring the rondo as the final movement in instrumental works. And like Haydn and Mozart he often combined elements of sonata form and rondo form. He did so in the finale of his Piano Sonata in A Major.

| SONATA FORM | Exposition | | | Development | Recapitulation | | | Coda |
|---|---|---|---|---|---|---|---|---|
| | Melodic area 1 | Modulatory passage | Melodic area 2 | | Melodic area 1 | Modulatory passage | Melodic area 2 | |
| **RONDO FORM** | A | B | | A | C | A | B′ | | A? |
| **KEY** (I = A) | I | I–V | V–I | I | i | I | I–V | I | I |
| **MEASURES** | 1–16 | 17–26 | 27–40 | 41–56 | 57–100 | 101–116 | 117–124 | 125–136 | 136–188 |

The rondo theme is in rounded binary form, but at 16 measures (and without repeats) it is much shorter than the binary melodies that Haydn used in the finale of his *Joke* Quartet (72 measures, taking the repeats into account; see Anthology 19) and the slow movement of his Symphony No. 97 (44 measures, including written-out repeats; see Anthology 24). With its elegant syncopated melody, predominantly two-part texture, appoggiaturas, an accompanimental pattern that alludes to the old Alberti bass, and even its unusual tempo indication (grazioso), this tune is ostentatiously galant. Did Beethoven intend some kind of parody? Was the young composer making affectionate fun of his elders? Or was he taking a nostalgic look back at the musical style of his childhood?

The first episode begins with a passage that could have served as the bridge in a sonata-form exposition, and indeed this passage serves exactly the same purpose: to modulate to the dominant in preparation for the melody in E major that begins at measure 27. But instead of the closing material that we would expect in a sonata-form movement, a transition leads back to the tonic and a second statement of the rondo theme.

The enormous second episode (C) resembles the rondo theme in being in rounded binary form (this time with repeats), but otherwise it presents a completely different expressive world. The minor mode, heavy chords, and staccato triplets played (for the most part) *fortissimo* anticipate the heroic style of Beethoven's middle period. The third statement of the rondo theme constitutes the beginning of the recapitulation. It continues with the rondo's third episode, which retraces the road taken in the first episode while staying in the tonic.

Throughout his life, codas offered Beethoven the opportunity to look back on entire movements and to develop their material further. He rarely turned down that opportunity. Here he transformed what at first appears to be the last statement of the rondo theme (beginning at m. 136) into a vast coda by interrupting it after four measures with music that takes the theme into new tonal territory. Later he reintroduced the staccato triplets from the central minor-mode episode (m. 162); by using these triplets in a transition back to the rondo theme, he reconciled the movement's most diverse elements. He finally allowed the rondo theme, beginning again at measure 174, to reach a cadence in A major, signaling the coda's (and the movement's) approaching end. When it arrives, it does so with the half-note appoggiatura from the end of the theme, now serving as the end of the movement as a whole.

## 27

JOSEPH HAYDN (1732–1809)

# The Seasons: *Hier treibt ein dichter Kreis* and *Hört das laute Getön*

## 1801

From Joseph Haydn, *Die Jahreszeiten*. Piano arrangement with English text by Rich Heuberger (Vienna: Universal Edition).

Schon flieht____ der auf-ge-spreng-te

Hirsch; ihm ren-nen, ihm ren-nen die Dog-gen und Rei-ter

Er flieht, er

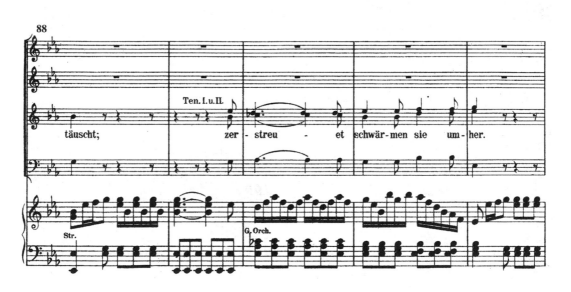

137 ganz erschöpft, er _ lie - - get nun___ das schnel-le Tier.

Sein na-hes

144 En-de kün-digt an; des tö-nen-den Er-zes Ju-bel - lied,___ der

150 freu-di-gen Jä - ger Sie - ges-laut: Ha - la - -

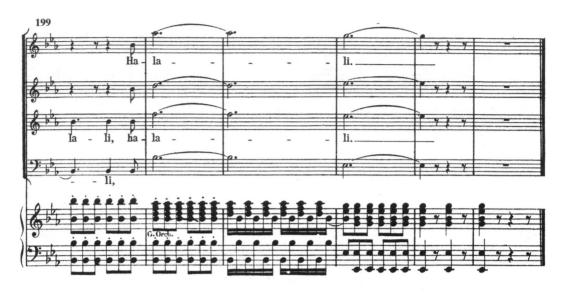

RECITATIVE, LUKAS

### LUKAS

| | |
|---|---|
| Hier treibt ein dichter Kreis | *Here a contracting circle* |
| Die Hasen aus dem Lager auf. | *drives the hares from their burrows.* |
| Von allen Seiten hergedrängt | *Forced to the center from every side,* |
| Hilft ihnen keine Flucht. | *they find no way to escape.* |
| Schon fallen sie und liegen bald | *Now they fall down, and soon they lie* |
| In Reihen freudig hingezählt. | *in rows, to be happily counted up.* |

### CHORUS OF COUNTRY FOLK AND OF HUNTERS

### MEN

| | |
|---|---|
| Hört das laute Getön, | *Listen! Listen to the loud noise* |
| Das dort im Walde klinget! | *that echoes through the woods.* |

### WOMEN

| | |
|---|---|
| Welch ein lautes Getön | *What a loud noise* |
| Durchklingt den ganzen Wald! | *makes the whole forest reverberate.* |

### ALL

| | |
|---|---|
| Es ist der gellenden Hörner Schall | *It is the shrill sound of horns,* |
| Der gierigen Hunde Gebelle. | *the barking of eager hounds.* |

MEN

Schon flieht der aufgesprengte Hirsch;
Ihm rennen die Doggen und Reiter nach.

*Already flees the startled stag;*
*the dogs and riders pursue him.*

ALL

Er flieht! Er flieht! O wie er sich streckt!
Ihm rennen die Doggen und Reiter nach.
O wie er springt! O wie er sich streckt!
Da bricht er aus den Gesträuchen hervor
Und läuft über Feld in das Dickicht hinein.

*He flies, he flies! Oh, how he bounds!*
*The dogs and riders pursue him.*
*Oh, how he jumps! Oh, how he bounds!*
*Now he breaks out of the bushes*
*and runs over the field and into the thicket.*

MEN

Jetzt hat er die Hunde getäuscht;
Zerstreuet schwärmen sie umher.

*Now he has deceived the dogs;*
*dispersed, they wander here and there.*

ALL

Die Hunde sind zerstreut;
Sie schwärmen hin und her.

*The dogs are dispersed;*
*they wander here and there.*

HUNTERS

Tajo, tajo, tajo!

*Tallyho! Tallyho! Tallyho!*

MEN

Der Jäger Ruf, der Hörner Klang
Versammelt auf's neue sie.

*The hunters' cry, the horns' clangor*
*assemble them again.*

HUNTERS

Ho, ho! Tajo! Tajo!

*Ho, ho, Tallyho! Tallyho!*

MEN AND WOMEN

Mit doppeltem Eifer stürzet nun
Der Haufe vereint auf die Fährte los.

*With renewed zeal the pack*
*rushes off together on the trail.*

HUNTERS

Tajo! Tajo! Tajo!

*Tallyho! Tallyho! Tallyho!*

WOMEN

Von seinen Feinden eingeholt,
An Mut und Kräften ganz erschöpft,
Erlieget nun das schnelle Tier.

*Overtaken by his enemies,*
*his spirit and strength exhausted,*
*the swift deer now falls.*

MEN

| Sein nahes Ende kündigt an | *His approaching end is proclaimed* |
|---|---|
| Des tönenden Erzes Jubellied, | *by the rejoicing song of the resounding brass* |
| Der freudigen Jäger Siegeslaut: | *and the joyful hunters' victorious shout:* |

HUNTERS

| Halali, halali, halali!* | *Halali, halali, halali!* |
|---|---|

WOMEN

| Den Tod des Hirsches kündigt an | *The stag's death is proclaimed* |
|---|---|
| Des tönenden Erzes Jubellied, | *by the rejoicing song of the resounding brass* |
| Der freudigen Jäger Siegeslaut: | *and the joyful hunters' victorious shout:* |

HUNTERS

| Halali, halali, halali! | *Halali, halali, halali!* |
|---|---|

ALL

| Den Tod des Hirsches kündigt an | *The stag's death is proclaimed* |
|---|---|
| Des tönenden Erzes Jubellied, | *by the rejoicing song of the resounding brass* |
| Der freudigen Jäger Siegeslaut: | *and the joyful hunters' victorious shout:* |
| Halali, halali, halali! | *Halali, halali, halali!* |

* "Halali" is a traditional hunter's cry announcing the animal's death.

The success that greeted Joseph Haydn's late oratorio *The Creation* when it was first performed in 1798 led his admirers, and especially Gottfried van Swieten, his literary collaborator, to urge him to undertake another oratorio. Now in his late sixties, Haydn was as eager as Swieten to capitalize on his sudden popularity as a composer of oratorio. They worked together to develop a musical dramatization of *The Seasons*, a poem in four books by the Scottish poet James Thomson.

Thomson's poem is concerned primarily with the unfolding of the seasons in the countryside; he describes the labors and pleasures of the peasants and the changing weather and landscapes in which they pass the year. Haydn's *The Seasons* takes its four-part form (beginning with spring and ending with winter) and its rustic settings and characters from Thomson's poem. But in its alternation of arias, ensembles, and choruses, and its frequent use of instrumental music to depict details of the text, *The Seasons* is very much a sequel to *The Creation*, which itself stood in a direct line of succession from George Frideric Handel's oratorios.

Fall is the main season for hunting, and given the importance of the hunt for eighteenth-century courts and nobility, it is not surprising that Haydn devoted to it a major portion of the third part of *The Seasons*. In keeping with his focus on simple country folk, the hunting begins with a rustic roundup of hares, described by the peasant Lukas in a recitative in which the accompanying strings beautifully evoke the animals' panicky attempts to escape their captors.

A much noisier, more colorful hunt interrupts the peasants, as noblemen on horseback follow their dogs through the countryside. Even this aristocratic hunt is seen from the peasants' point of view, at least at first. Haydn described the choir that sings *Hört das laute Getön* as representing "country folk and hunters," but it is not until more than halfway through the chorus that the hunters have anything to say ("Tallyho!").

Instead of a conventional structure involving a large-scale opposition of tonic and dominant keys and melodies that, in returning after intervening music, imbue a movement with a sense of unity, Haydn made this movement a kind of free fantasy whose unpredictability mirrors the unpredictability of the hunt itself. For his musical material he depended primarily on the horn signals that eighteenth-century mounted hunters used to communicate with one another. So that no member of his audience could possibly miss the point, he had the music begin with four horns by themselves, playing in unison the signal traditionally used to announce the beginning of a hunt.

The country folk respond first to the signals broadcast across the countryside by the horns and barking of hunting dogs. (The slurred three-note scale fragments imitating the barking of dogs at mm. 34–35 and 40–42 recall Christoph Gluck's evocation of Cerberus in *Orfeo ed Euridice*; see Anthology 9.) At measure 44 the chorus turns its attention from the noise of the hunt to the quarry: a stag depicted by the orchestra with running sixteenth notes. Later, to show the deer leaping, the orchestra plays a disjunct passage in which groups of sixteenth notes alternate with groups of eighth notes.

Haydn transformed the hunt into something extraordinary by using tonality to dramatize the next turn of events. The stag escapes his pursuers by plunging into a thicket. The music, hitherto limited to D major (with occasional moves toward the dominant, A) by the horns in D that dominate the first part of the chorus, suddenly moves to the parallel minor and then on to G minor and E♭ major. None of these modulations is unusual in itself, but the move from D to E♭—a musical escape from the tonic—is as surprising as the deer's disappearance. (Recall the similar effect of Mozart's Fiordiligi, in a duet in A major, attempting to escape from Ferrando's advances by modulating to C major; see Anthology 21.) The surprise is compounded by the reappearance of two of the horns, whose players, by changing crooks during the modulatory passage, have transformed their instruments from horns in D to horns in E♭.

Urged by the hunters (whom the choir portrays here for the first time), the dogs regroup and finally catch up with the now exhausted stag, and the sopranos and altos, in a quiet passage that begins in A♭, encourage us to feel a moment of pity for the poor beast. But his actual death—presumably torn apart by the dogs—passes without poetic or musical elaboration. It is characteristic of the eighteenth century that Haydn and Swieten ignored the hunt's violent and bloody climax, preferring to end this chorus with a celebration of its successful conclusion.

The chorus ends in E♭, tonally far from where it began. Haydn had juxtaposed passages a half step apart in the Piano Sonata No. 52 in E♭ Major (see Anthology 25), with its slow central movement in E♮. But he restored a sense of balance and normalcy by returning to E♭ for the third and final movement. In this chorus he went much further, breaking one of the most basic rules of Western music. In doing so, did he hope to suggest the distance traveled by the hunters? Or did he want listeners to think that the excitement and confusion of the hunt caused the hunters to forget where they began? Perhaps, on a more practical level, he simply wanted to avoid forcing his horn players to change their crooks a second time.

# Symphony No. 3 in E♭ Major *(Sinfonia eroica)*: Movement 2, *Marcia funebre*

## 1804

From Ludwig van Beethoven, *First, Second, and Third Symphonies* (New York: Dover Publications, Inc.).

Emerging from the emotional crisis that Beethoven endured in 1802, his Third Symphony was completed in 1804 and published two years later. Although he originally intended to name the symphony after Napoleon or at least to dedicate it to him, Napoleon's crowning himself emperor in 1804 caused Beethoven to change his mind. When the symphony was published, dedicated to his generous patron Prince Joseph Lobkowitz, it was under the title *Sinfonia eroica, composta per festeggiare il sovvenire di un gran Uomo* (Heroic Symphony, Composed to Celebrate the Memory of a Great Man).

Beethoven labeled the second movement *Marcia funebre* (Funeral March), but efforts to connect the movement with the death of one person are probably as misguided as attempts to identify the "great man" of the title page. The *Eroica* is about heroism (including that of Beethoven himself) and greatness in general; it is not a portrait of any one man.

Beethoven's sketches show that in the early stages of composition of his Third Symphony he considered the idea of making the slow movement an Adagio in C major. But he rejected this plan in favor of a vast, somber funeral march in C minor. This was a revolutionary idea, not only because the incorporation of a funeral march into a symphony was apparently unprecedented, but also because any kind of symphonic slow movement in the minor mode was rare, at least in the works of Mozart and Haydn. In the form of a rondo, the *Marcia funebre* consists of a march in C minor (**A** in the diagram below) presented three times (the second time only in fragmentary form and the third time much altered) in alternation with two episodes—the first in C major and the second a fugato in F minor—and followed by a coda.

| FORM | A | B | A' | C | A'' | Coda |
|---|---|---|---|---|---|---|
| KEY (i = C MINOR) | i | I | i | iv–v | v–i | i |
| MEASURES | 1–68 | 69–104 | 105–114 | 114–154 | 154–209 | 209–247 |

The march proper is in rounded binary form. The first part, modulating to the relative major, Eb, is played once. The second part, starting in Eb and working its way back to C minor, is played twice, first with the strings taking the lead (mm. 17–36) and then with the winds (mm. 37–56). A codetta (a coda-like passage that serves to reinforce the end of a section of a larger movement) brings the march to a close.

### March (corresponding to A in the diagram above)

| FORM | First Part | | Second Part | | | Codetta |
|---|---|---|---|---|---|---|
| | A | B | A' | B | A' | |
| KEY (i=C MINOR) | i–III | III | iv–i | III | iv–i | i |
| MEASURES | 1–16 | 17–30 | 31–36 | 37–50 | 51–56 | 56–68 |

Sixteenth-note triplets dominate the first episode, a through-composed passage in C major (mm. 69–104). In the context of a funeral march, such triumphant music suggests the idea of apotheosis: either in its literal sense (the deification of the dead hero) or figuratively (the glorification of the hero in the memories of the living). But the triumph is short-lived: it leads to a return of the funeral march in the tonic (m. 105).

This second statement of the march is soon interrupted (m. 114) by a magnificent double fugato in F minor. (A fugato is a fugue-like passage within a larger, predominantly homophonic movement; a double fugato begins with two subjects simultaneously.) One of the subjects, first played by violas and bassoons, prominently sounds the expressive interval of the augmented second. The other subject, first played by the second violins, begins with a scalar ascent of a fourth: an inversion of a motive first heard at the beginning of the second part of the march (mm. 17–18). The fugato reaches a climax at measure 145, in the form of a series of dissonant suspensions over a dominant pedal. (Christoph Gluck had used a similar passage to similar effect in the opening Maestoso of his underworld scene in *Orfeo ed Euridice* in 1762; see Anthology 9, mm. 12–15.)

The funeral march returns in G minor, instead of the expected tonic C minor (m. 154), and is almost immediately interrupted by a *fortissimo* blast, as if in violent protest against the wrong key. When the march begins again (m. 173), now in the correct key, an oboe and clarinet in octaves carry the melody. It ends with a deceptive cadence (mm. 208–9) that launches the coda.

Although the coda begins by hinting at the keys of A♭ and D♭ major, a B♮ in the bass at measure 218 pulls the music back to the tonic C minor. The coda ends with the first violins playing the first eight measures of the march, but broken up into small fragments. Haydn did something similar at the end of his *Joke* Quartet (see Anthology 19). But the effect of that ending is worlds apart from what Beethoven achieved here: an expression of incoherent, inconsolable grief.

# String Quartet in C Major, Op. 59, No. 3 ("Razumovsky"): Movement 4

## 1806

From Ludwig van Beethoven, *Complete String Quartets* (New York: Dover Publications, Inc.).

Almost exactly 25 years after Haydn transformed the string quartet with his Opus 33 (written in 1781; see Anthology 19), Beethoven produced an equally revolutionary set of string quartets. Count Andrey Kyrillovich Razumovsky, the Russian ambassador in Vienna, was an enthusiastic patron of instrumental music and a lover of the string quartet. He sponsored one of Vienna's earliest professional quartet ensembles, led by the violinist Ignaz Schuppanzigh, and commissioned Beethoven to write three quartets for it. Thus he encouraged Beethoven, who had written no quartets since Opus 18 (1798–1801), to return to this genre in the middle of his heroic period.

Although string quartets made up of professional musicians performed quite frequently in public concerts in London in the 1780s, in Vienna both the genre and the ensemble were more closely associated with private music-making. Even when professional musicians played string quartets, they generally did so for their own pleasure. By commissioning Beethoven to write quartets for a professional ensemble, Razumovsky encouraged him to redefine the Viennese string quartet as a genre for listeners as well as players.

The three "Razumovsky" Quartets, Op. 59, constitute a monumental trilogy reminiscent, in some respects, of Mozart's last three symphonies. Like Mozart's last symphony, the *Jupiter* (K. 551), Op. 59, No. 3 is in C major and culminates in an imposing finale that explores fugal techniques within the context of sonata form.

Beethoven's decision to make the third movement of Op. 59, No. 3 an old-fashioned minuet, instead of a scherzo, left this quartet without the frenetic movement that his admirers must have expected of him. In the finale he supplied it. An expression of exuberance and joy, this movement, labeled Allegro molto, brings to a satisfying and applause-generating conclusion not only the Quartet in C Major but the "Razumovsky" trilogy as a whole.

As is often the case with sonata-form movements in which neither the exposition nor the development–recapitulation is repeated, it is impossible to say exactly where the exposition ends and the development begins. Beethoven blurred the boundaries between the first part and the second, and between the second part and the coda, with transition passages. The diagram that follows assigns the transitions to the end of the exposition (ending on the dominant of E♭) and recapitulation (ending on the dominant of A♭); but these transitions can just as easily be heard as constituting the beginning of the development and coda.

| FORM | First Part | Second Part | | Coda |
|---|---|---|---|---|
| | Exposition | Development | Recapitulation | |
| KEY (I = C) | I–V–V/♭III | ♭III ∿∿∿ | I–V/♭VI | ♭VI–I |
| MEASURES | 1–92 | 93–209 | 210–305 | 306–429 |

The movement begins with a manically energetic fugato that ends abruptly as soon as all four voices have entered. Beethoven coordinated the successive entry of the parts with a massive crescendo that continues until a strong cadence in tonic C at measure 47 signals the end of the first melodic area.

In the modulatory passage that follows, homophonic textures almost orchestral in their richness (appropriate for a large room holding a numerous audience) might make us wonder if Beethoven has abandoned the learned style for good. A second melodic area in the expected key of G major brings with it a return to polyphony, but not the fugal style with which the movement began. For that we have to wait until the huge development, beginning with (or preceded by) a modulation to E♭ major. In an unpredictable alteration of contrapuntal and homophonic passages, Beethoven explores a wide variety of keys, with an emphasis on the distant realm of C♯ minor. The recapitulation brings back the fugato in full, but now with a new countersubject in half notes.

The cadential material, now in C major, leads to a coda of vast proportions, even longer than the development. Although it starts in A♭ major, it soon returns to C and stays there. The last 41 measures bring back the long crescendo with which the movement began, but this time celebrating the pleasures of finality. This ending demands applause. It reminds us that Beethoven, in writing such music, and Razumovsky, in assembling and paying the ensemble for which Beethoven wrote it, helped to transform the string quartet.

# READING AN ORCHESTRAL SCORE

## CLEFS

The music for some instruments is written in clefs other than the familiar treble and bass. In the following example, middle C is shown in the four clefs used in orchestral scores:

The alto clef is primarily used in viola parts. The tenor clef is employed for cello, bassoon, and trombone parts when these instruments play in a high register.

## TRANSPOSING INSTRUMENTS

The music for some instruments is customarily written at a pitch different from their actual sound. The following list, with examples, shows the transposing instruments that appear in this volume.

| Instrument | Transposition | Written note | Actual sound |
|---|---|---|---|
| Trumpet in D | sounds a major second higher than written | | |
| Trumpet in C | sounds as written | | |
| Clarinet in B♭ | sounds a major second lower than written | | |
| Double Bass | sounds an octave lower than written | | |
| Horn in G | sounds a fourth lower than written | | |
| Horn in F | sounds a fifth lower than written | | |
| Horn in E♭ | sounds a major sixth lower than written | | |
| Horn in D | sounds a minor seventh lower than written | | |
| Horn in C Double bass | sound an octave lower than written | | |

# INSTRUMENT NAMES AND ABBREVIATIONS

## WOODWINDS

| English | Italian | German |
|---------|---------|--------|
| Flute (Fl.) | Flauto (Fl.) | Flöte (Fl.) |
| Oboe (Ob.) | Oboe (Ob.) | Hoboe (Hb.) |
| Clarinet (Cl.) | Clarinetto (Cl.) | Klarinette (Klar.) |
| Bassoon (Bsn.) | Fagotto (Fag.) | Fagott (Fag.) |
| Contrabassoon (C. bsn.) | Contrafagotto (C. fag., Contra fag.) | Kontrafagott (K-fg.) |

## BRASS

| English | Italian | German |
| --- | --- | --- |
| Horn (Hn.) | Corno (Cor.) | Horn (Hr.) |
| Trumpet (Tpt.) | Tromba (Tr., Tr-ba), Clarino | Trompete (Trpt.) |
| Trombone (Trb.) | Trombone (Trb.) | Posaune (Pos.) |

## PERCUSSION

| English | Italian | German |
| --- | --- | --- |
| Kettledrums (K. D.) | Timpani (Timp., Tp.) | Pauken (Pk.) |

## STRINGS

| English | Italian | German |
| --- | --- | --- |
| Violin (Vln.) | Violino (Viol.) | Violine (Viol.) |
| Viola (Va.) | Viola (Vla.) | Bratsche (Br.) |
| Violoncello, Cello (Vc.) | Violoncello (Cll.) | Violoncello (Vc.) |
| Double bass (D. bs.) | Contrabasso (C. B.), Basso | Kontrabaβ (Kb.) |

## KEYBOARD INSTRUMENTS

| English | Italian | German |
| --- | --- | --- |
| Clavichord | Clavicordo | Klavichord, Klavier |
| Harpsichord | Cembalo | Cembalo, Klavier, Flügel |
| Piano, Fortepiano | Pianoforte (Pft.), Fortepiano | Klavier, Flügel |

## NOTE NAMES

| English | Italian | German |
| --- | --- | --- |
| C | do | C |
| C♯ | do diesis | Cis |
| D♭ | re bemolle | Des |
| D | re | D |
| D♯ | re diesis | Dis |
| E♭ | mi bemolle | Es |
| E | mi | E |
| E♯ | mi diesis | Eis |
| F♭ | fa bemolle | Fes |
| F | fa | F |
| F♯ | fa diesis | Fis |
| G♭ | sol bemolle | Ges |
| G | sol | G |
| G♯ | sol diesis | Gis |
| A♭ | la bemolle | As |
| A | la | A |
| B♭ | si bemolle | B |
| B | si | H |
| B♯ | si diesis | His |
| C♭ | do bemolle | Ces |

# APPENDIX 3

# GLOSSARY OF PERFORMANCE INDICATIONS

**a**   at, by

**adagio**   a slow tempo

**al, alla**   to the, at the

**allegretto**   a moderately fast tempo

**allegro (allo.)**   a rapid tempo

**andante**   a moderately slow tempo

**arco**   played with the bow

**capo**   beginning

**corda**   string

**crescendo (cresc., cres)**   becoming louder

**da**   from

**dal, dalla**   from the

**decrescendo (decresc.)**   becoming softer

**del, della**   of the

**di**   of

**diminuendo (dim.)**   becoming softer

**dolce**   sweetly

**fine**   end

**forte (f, for)**   loud

**fortissimo (ff, for^mo)**   very loud

**grave**   heavy, strong

**grazioso**   graceful

**il**   the

**larghetto**   the diminutive of *largo*, somewhat faster than *largo*

**largo**   a very slow tempo

**legato**   smooth

**ma**   but

**maestoso**   majestic

**maggiore**   major

**marcato (marc.)**   with emphasis

**mezzo, mezza**   half

**minore**   minor

**moderato (modto.)**   at a moderate tempo

**molto**   very much

**mosso**   rapid

**non**   not

**pianissimo (pp, pssmo)**   very soft

**piano (p, pia)**   soft

**più**   more

**pizzicato (pizz.)**   plucked

**poco**   little

**presto**   a very quick tempo

**recitativo (recvo.)**   a singing style imitating speech

**segno**   sign

**sempre**   always

**sostenuto**  sustained
**sotto**  under
**staccato (stacc.)**  detached
**sul, sulla**  on the
**troppo**  too much

**tutti**  all
**un, una**  a, one
**vivace**  lively
**voce**  voice